ETHICS AND TECHNOLOGY

Ethical Choices in the Age of Pervasive Technology

Edited by:

Jorge Nef
Jokelee Vanderkop
Henry Wiseman
The University of Guelph

WALL & THOMPSON
Toronto

Canadian Cataloguing in Publication Data

Main entry under title:
Ethics and technology

Includes bibliographical references.
ISBN 0–921332–34–3

1. Technology—Moral and ethical aspects.
I. Nef, J. (Jorge), 1942–   .   II. Vanderkop, J.
(Jokelee).   III. Wiseman, Henry.

BJ59.E74   1989   170   C98–095199–3

Special acknowledgement and thanks to the International Development Research Centre, Ottawa, for their cooperation and financial support.

Cover Artwork designed by Chris Boyadijian, Publications and Printing Services, University of Guelph.

Art direction by Gabrielle Duval, Publications and Printing Services, University of Guelph.

Illustrations by Ian Cauthery, Publications and Printing Services, University of Guelph. Photographs courtesy of the International Development Research Centre and the National Research Council, Ottawa.

ISBN 0–921332–34–3
Printed in Canada.
1 2 3 4 5   93 92 91 90 89

Table of Contents

FOREWORD *Henry Wiseman*

The Challenges of Technology

In the 20th century, many exciting and powerful technologies have transformed the global configuration and the way of life for all humanity. Historically, technologies have taken us from the stone age to the nuclear age, and are propelling us into a future where they may be as hazardous to life and the world as they may be beneficial.

Shall we trust our future to a drifting interplay of forces, to the genius of technological invention and mechanistic social design, or will society chart the course so that technologies will truly serve the needs of humanity at large?

Our concern is not merely to understand and appreciate past and possible future technological choices and their consequences. We need to assess the broader effects of diverse technologies on national and international issues as well as in more specific areas such as bioethics, medicine, the media, communication, governmental policies, education and industrial innovation. Although ethical and moral issues in each field are very different, there are marked similarities. In short, we are looking to substantive guidelines for future planning and action.

The possibility, if not the promise, of sustainable economic, political and social development for all humanity exists, but it is by no means assured. In such a society, individuals would live in dignity and justice with their basic needs satisfied. If we base our convictions and our efforts on the universal social values of equality, human rights, freedom, and individual and collective development, and make careful use of human creativity, natural resources and technological innovation, we may eventually achieve a vibrant, creative and compassionate world.

In the past 5000 years moments of inspiration, revelation, and creative genius have produced the wheel and the printing press, have tamed water and fire to generate energy, and have created large-scale manufacturing industries. These have forever altered the nature of our existence in thought and behaviour. However, the most astonishing leaps have taken place in the last 50 years with people taking to the air, developing nuclear power and computers, and venturing into space. All this has resulted in the quality of life being improved in some parts of the world from a primitive struggle for survival to a lifestyle characterized by longevity and abundance, ease of work, leisure, and a cornucopia of opportunities and pleasures. Yet, other parts of the world have fared less well or have actually been disadvantaged. Individual insights from charismatic leaders and scientists and collective insights of ordinary people have forged great social contracts like the Charter of the United Nations and have shaped the way we see ourselves. *And this we have come to call progress.*

Over time, we have come to depend on technologies for the solution to many of our problems. The popular and political imagination is captivated by the belief that they are an autonomous and neutral historical force. We think that new technologies will rectify the old, and that the marketplace will continue to fuel the development of more and still better technologies and harmoniously keep all things in balance. This is the age of the virtual deification of technology. *And this too we have come to call progress.*

Much of the miraculous inventiveness of technology that we perceive as "making all things possible" has come to us at great cost. Majestic forests are being replaced by barren deserts while our once crystal waters and blue skies have become the sinks for chemical pollutants. Technological advances have led to extreme social and economic disruptions. This has aggravated the schisms between the developed and developing worlds, dividing rich and poor even more. Technology has also abetted arms races. The next season in the promised land may be no more than nuclear winter. *And this we surely cannot call progress.*

We can no longer rely on the misguided view that the uncritical investment in so-called neutral technologies will naturally bring about the best of all possible worlds. Nor should we attempt to restrain scientific enquiry, technological innovation and industrial development because of misguided fears. The best of all possible worlds must surely be based on human spirit, human values and a profound concern for all life, the environment and the earth itself. There are choices to be made. Men and women everywhere and from all walks of life will decide how we can best use the magnificent potential of technology to enshrine and realize our hopes for the sustainable development of a just and equitable world.

We have for too long examined these problems in isolation. The time has now come for mutual enquiry and consultation to strengthen our understanding and to formulate common approaches to these most serious and troublesome issues in this age of technology.

This volume is a first, but necessary, effort to forge a foundation upon which diverse and sectarian interests can be brought together. Each article highlights the relationship between social values and technologies and how this relationship affects progress. Technological progress, however, presents three major challenges.

The *first* is the challenge to the social values and ethical foundations of all societies. Whether based on faith, philosophy, historical experience or a synthesis of all three, these foundations have been disrupted by the clash between economic growth and a sustainable future as exemplified by consumerism and pollution, technologically driven health services versus nutrition and sanitation, and intensive agriculture and soil degradation. These and other equally serious issues are addressed in these articles.

The *second* dramatic consequence of our technological era is specialization. The explosion of knowledge and functions has narrowed the range of expertise within government and the private sector and within academia itself. The gap between the natural sciences and social sciences and humanities, despite protestations to the contrary, are, I believe, wider than ever before. Each carries out its specific tasks with little cohesion between them and little ethical concern for the implications of these tasks. The need for mutual regard and consultation is absolutely critical. Yet this remains an extremely difficult undertaking.

The *third* and most critical factor is the velocity of change. The number of events which can be induced in a very short period of time has multiplied. Computer dominated business, defence, and industrial production are cases in point. For similar reasons, the time lapse between cause and consequence has been drastically reduced. The immediate and widespread dissemination of any event— economic, political, environmental, or military—may cause instant reverberations around the world.

With events happening so quickly, the hiatus between cause and consequence makes it difficult for appropriate ethical judgements to be brought to bear upon a situation. Competing interests, whether economic, political, environmental or otherwise, generate crises. But the ethical questions and enquiry arise only after the deleterious effects have occurred. For instance, the scientist may argue that scientific research, pure and simple, is the pursuit of knowledge and that others should be responsible for the political and ethical judgements. Using the same rational, the technologist applies his skills to build a prototype while the industri- alist manufactures and markets the product in the pursuit of profits and economic efficiency. In turn, governments encourage research and development and use existing products to accomplish political interests defined as "national goals." Throughout the entire chain of events, the participants have concerned themselves with the pursuit of knowledge, skills, wealth and power. Serious ethical consider- ations have been largely absent.

Should the ethical issues and the responsibility to consider them be left to the last critical moment? Or should those who contribute to each stage of development be obliged to at least consider the ethical consequences of their actions? These are not simple questions; but in a technologically instantaneous world, such questions can no longer be avoided. They apply to almost every field from research, defence, industrial production, health, agriculture, environment to communications, edu- cation, finance and law.

Humans have been much more clever in producing technological "artifacts" than in regulating the way in which they are used. Is their wisdom deficient? Or is the world driven by a neutral technological motor over which humanity has no control? I do not believe that either is true. Humankind is certainly capable of applying its wisdom to a better understanding of the relationship between techno- logical development and ethical judgement. This collection of articles has been written to enable us to embark on such an enquiry.

DR. HENRY WISEMAN is a political scientist and Chair of the Conference, *"Ethical Choices in the Age of Pervasive Technology,"* University of Guelph, October 25–29, 1989.

PREFACE   *The Editors*

Some Necessary Explanations

This edited volume is an outgrowth of the 1989 Global Conference on "Ethical Choices in the Age of Pervasive Technology" held at the University of Guelph. During the early planning stages, the Executive Committee decided to produce a series of short, concise, and provocative articles on the themes of the Conference to provide basic "food for thought" for the workshops and panel discussions. Thus, the idea of a pre-conference publication came into being.

In order to go beyond the confines of one single event, however, we decided to turn this preconference publication into an introductory-level book that would reach a wider audience: policy-makers, business people, academics, teachers, students, and the interested public at large. Our interest was to create a work that had the depth of coverage appropriate to a serious intellectual pursuit while still appealing to a large interdisciplinary constituency. In other words, we wanted to inform the layperson while not offending the expert.

In general, the present volume follows the framework of the Conference. Six major problem-areas are identified: the global ecosystem, the resource base, the economy, society, polity and culture. In each one of these units a number of specific themes are discussed which illustrate the more fundamental ethical dilemmas.

Unit I lays the conceptual and historical foundations of the book. J. Nef's article on perspectives and definitions examines technology as a human and cultural system. F. Knelman traces the relationships between technology and human history leading to the present crisis of values. Schtivelman and Russell tackle the complex interconnections between technology, sustainable development and human resources, where the latter hold the key to adaptation and technological progress. P. Durbin's examines various inscribed paradigms of the linkages between technology and values, in particular the question of "activism" and responsibility in the North American context.

Unit II deals with global issues of survival, especially with environmental concerns, peace and security, and global development. V. Thomas discusses the threats, as well as the opportunities, posed by technological development to the complex and delicate global ecological balance. G. Lindsey and G. Pearson analyze the contributions and possible drawbacks of technological developments in maintaining peace and security among nations. N. Cebotarev looks at the ethical void present in the standard relationship between technology and international development and suggests alternative ways for reconstructing this relationship.

Unit III concentrates upon that part of the ecosystem which is exploited as a productive resource. The key issue here is that of sustainability of the resource base. Two areas are discussed. T. Turner treats the question of ethics in energy technology from a broad political economy perspective while F. Hurnik and H. Lehman approach the association between technology, values, and agriculture.

Unit IV focuses on the economy and economic efficiency. D. Taylor and T. Phillips examine ethical and technological choices in the context of economic rationality. F. Evers centers on technology and ethics from the perspective of business organizations: the side of production and capital. E. Bernard, in turn, looks at the other side of the equation: labour, ethics, and technological change. M. Anandakrishnan explores the issues posed by the apparent contradictions between equity, distribution, and technological options, both between rich and poor nations and rich and poor peoples.

Unit V deals with society, more specifically with quality of life and social justice. D. Roy discusses the specific case of health and the life sciences with regards to the ethics of knowledge and power. M. McDonald looks at the power of experts and the ethical problems emerging from the concentration of "know-how."

Unit VI discusses the ethical problems relating to technology and the state. M. Bailey concentrates on the issue of reproductive freedom as it is affected by technology and politics, while J. de la Mothe delves into the intricate issue of regulation of science and technology and its impact on ethical choice.

Unit VII is devoted to the study of cultural "software" as it pertains to ethics and technology. Several aspects are considered. One is the problem of innovation, communication, and the media presented by J. Meisel. The second, by C. Beck, focuses on the question of technology, education, and learning. J. Shute's essay explores the relationship between technology, ethics, and human resource development, rounding out some of the arguments presented in the introduction by Schtivelman and Russell. This unit ends up with a piece by A. Abraham and J. Mullin which examines the association between technological innovation, research, and development in general.

The concluding unit examines two sets of ethically significant consequences of scientific and technological development. The work by G. Erasmus looks at some of the "victims" of technologically-induced development: native peoples and the "powerless." J. Jørgenson takes a broad macro perspective and looks at the global interdependence resulting from modern technology and its social and material constraints.

Needless to say, the authors do not pretend that this volume is a final product. Rather, it is designed to raise questions and to motivate discussion for a deeper examination of the many issues sampled here. If this happens, the editors would have accomplished their objective.

The Editors
Guelph, August 1989

UNIT I
INTRODUCTION

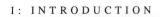

1

Jorge Nef

Technology Is About People: Some Basic Perspectives and Definitions

To label the contemporary era as a "Technological Age," or one of innovation and pervasive technology, is generally an accepted truism. The problem with common-sense labels, however, is that despite their descriptive value, they often cloud a deeper understanding of the complex reality they encapsulate. First, an oversimplification of this sort tends to close the mind to probing and fundamental questions about the long-range processes leading to the "here and now." Secondly, it precludes similar questions about probable futures and, most importantly, policy and individual choices regarding these futures. The "Technological Age" label conveys an image of a world compulsively driven by a "technological engine" whose effects harbour both promise and despair.

"Gifts of the Gods?"

The pace of scientific and technological change since the last century has *accelerated* dramatically. It has also become *global* in scope. Awesome breakthroughs such as nuclear power, computers or space travel and the multiplicity of household gadgets create a form of "cargo cult"[1] view of technology: unfathomable "gifts of the Gods." The ethical-moral basis for decision-making is subordinated to forces we cannot shape or direct. The process of technological change becomes an end-value in itself where "objective" technologies and "subjective" values are completely divorced from each other. Technology, therefore, is seen either as being amoral, "value-free" and creating its own sense of "higher" purpose or as something intrinsically immoral and even dangerous to our "humanness."

Technology as a System

One of the paradoxes of our times is that the more we take technology for granted, the less we seem to understand it. One could argue that we are simulta-

---

[1] By "cargo cult," we specifically mean the mystical-religious practices which emerged in the "stone age cultures" of Melanesia after the Second World War. This was a result of encounters between the indigenous cultures and the seemingly incomprehensible technological gadgetry (such as airplanes) brought by the Allies. It was an anomic response to culture shock. See Michael Walter, "Cult Movement and Community Development Associations: Evolution and Revolution in the Papua New Guinea Countryside," in Ralph Gerritsen, R.J. May and Michael Walter (eds.), *Road Toward Development. Cargo Cults, Community Groups and Self-Help Movements in Papua New Guinea,* (Canberra: Australian National University, Department of Political and Social Change, 1981), pp.81–105.

neously technologically-skilled and technologically-illiterate. There is a need to fill this gap which our educational system has pitifully failed to address. Irrespective of where one stands in the contemplation of modern technology, the impact of technological change in our lives is momentous. Most of us are aware of this in the "output" side, or receiving end. What we are most unaware of, however, is the overall process of technology generation and its consequences, not as a physical creation of gadgets alone, but as a *social* process.

This requires a *systemic* as opposed to a piecemeal perspective. In its broadest sense, technology refers to a society's set of practices, skills and instruments for problem-solving: the society's *know-how*. All societies, whether "traditional" or "modern," "developed" or "underdeveloped" possess such know-how. Jacques Ellul has defined technology, especially modern and Western technology, as *"the totality of methods rationally arrived at and having absolute efficiency* (for a given stage of development) in *every* field of human activity." [1] Technology can be viewed as an open system for problem-solving where five main elements interact:

  a. a *context* of problems and circumstances which the technology addresses
  b. a *culture* which gives meaning—purposes, feelings, cognitions and valuations—to such technological system,
  c. *structures* of groups and individuals with resources (tools), linked by networks of communications and charged with dealing with the problems affecting the system,
  d. a set of *processes* (procedures, practices and techniques) whereby groups and individuals attempt to solve problems, and
  e. *effects* or consequences of these actions upon the system.

From the above perspective, it is possible to argue that a technological system involves much more than *know-how about tools*. It encompasses as well the social structures and operations through which the tools are utilized as well as the value assumptions pertaining to those activities. That is, behind any piece of "hardware" there is a complex set of "soft" social practices (or *social technologies*) which make up the less visible—yet crucially important—human infrastructure upon which such hard technologies rest.[2] A tool, gadget or artifact (for instance, an automobile) is a *product* of a technological *process*. It results from the combination of resources (e.g. iron, silica, hydrocarbons) transformed by other tools (e.g. machinery) used by operators (designers, engineers, workers) who possess skills, techniques or know-how. It operates in a physical and resource environment as well as in an economic, social, political and cultural set up (e.g. the factory, the enterprise, finance, regulations, etc.) which affect the extent, scope and purpose of its application. In fact, a technology involves a series of *technological functions* in which the above-mentioned tools, operators, resources and culture are intertwined in complex organizational and social matrixes. The latter possess a built-in capacity for reproduction and expansion of know-how.

---

[1]

    Jacques Ellul, *The Technological Society*, (New York: Vintage Books, 1964), p.xxv.

[2]

    Cf. Mostafa K. Tolba, "Present Development Styles and Environmental Problems," *CEPAL Review*, (December 1985), pp.13–14.

A Conceptual Framework

From this same systemic and general perspective, we can see a society's technological matrix as encompassing six interrelated sub-systems along a continuum: the *ecology*, the *resource base*, the *economy*, the *society*, the *polity* and the *culture*.[1] Within each of these sub-systems we can identify a number of specific critical problem areas or issues. Environmental degradation, war, underdevelopment and pestilence threaten the ecology. Resource depletion and land exhaustion affect the resource base. Poverty and waste undermine the economy. Injustice and alienation affect the social order. Violence, repression and insecurity make the polity ungovernable while ignorance and prejudice disrupt cultural adaptation.

From an equally abstract and general perspective, we could identify a number of "desired" outcomes or "values" relating to the problems affecting the sub-systems. They are:

    a. environmental *survival,*

    b. *sustainability* of resources,

    c. economic *efficiency,*

    d. social *equity* and *justice,*

    e. political *liberty* and *order*

    f. cultural *enlightenment* and *accessibility.*

Technologies are instrumental to the attainment of desired outcomes. Some are more coherently and centrally defined, such as the broad label of engineering applied to resource extraction and transformation, or education as it pertains to culture-creation, distribution and maintenance. Others are much more fragmentary and unfocussed: commerce, business, finance, accounting in relation to the economy; social work, health care and law in relation to society; political practices, administration, warfare and control (enforcement) with reference to the polity. An area where it is still difficult to identify one or several technologies is that of the environment. We could describe these emerging technologies under the rubrics of conservation, peace-keeping, environmental medicine[2] and international development.

---

[1]

    For the purposes of our analysis, the ecology refers to the physical, natural environment or milieu. The resource base is that part of the natural environment which has been exploited for productive use. The economy refers to the structures and processes whereby resources are transformed and distributed to satisfy needs. This includes both "material" goods and services. The society incorporates the sum total of group interactions involving entities such as families, associations, and institutions. The polity or political system involves the society's structures and processes for conflict management. Culture refers to the set of beliefs, feelings, values, knowledge and, in general, ideas which shape the practices of all the subsystems.

[2]

    Environmental medicine refers to the series of practices to create and maintain a "healthy environment." This involves, among others, the control of epidemics and reduction of general health hazards, eradication of diseases etc. on a massive scale.

SYSTEM	THEMES *	PROBLEM	SCIENCE/ THEORY	TECHNOLOGY	VALUE
Global Eco-System	Environment Peace & Security Development	Degradation, War, Underdevelop-ment	Ecology Biology Geography	Conservarion Peace-keeping Medicine	Survival
Resources	Energy Agriculture	Depletion Exhaustion	Physics Chemistry Geology	Engineering Agronomy Veterinary	Sustainability
Economy	Theory Business Labour Equity	Poverty Waste	Economics	Business Accounting Commerce Finance	Efficiency
Society	Health Moral Choice	Injustice Alienation	Sociology	Social Work Health Care Recreation Law	Equity/ Justice (Well-being)
Polity	Law & State Reg-ulation	Violence Repression Insecurity Ungovern-ability	Politics	Government Administration Warfare Control	Liberty/ Order
Culture	Communications Learning H.R.D Research	Ignorance Prejudice	Philosophy	Education	Enlightenment Accessibility

* The themes constitute the basic chapter structure of the present volume

An important point must be raised here. Technologies are but the *means* by which desired outcomes are sought. Neither the technology (the know-how), nor the science (the know-what and know-why) can substitute for an ethical-normative foundation. Scientific inquiry as well as technical intervention in an area require the parallel development of an explicit ethical and value system related to the concrete "problems" extant in that area.

The quest for normative standards is ever more difficult since, in an increasingly interdependent world, the nation-state has ceased to be the ultimate "ethical community." The same is true with the erosion of more communitarian moral systems such as those of the family, the tribe or religion. The local (micro), the national (meso) and the global (macro) have become almost indistinguishable.

The tentative relationship mentioned is represented schematically in Figure 1-1.

The above remarks may help to stress a central tenet of our analysis: although we tend to separate the "hard" world of technology from the "soft" world of social practices, the two are inextricably linked. Both are part of a broad definition of culture in an anthropological sense.[1] Culture is not just an area of technological

---

[1] See Gordon Childe, *Man Makes Himself*, (New York: The New American Library, 1958), pp.20–36.

concern, it penetrates all the other dimensions given in the chart. Science and technology are as much a part of culture as are values, art and folklore.[1] We cannot fully understand the "utilitarian" components (i.e. gadgets) without understanding the complex set of beliefs, meanings and social practices which allow for the gadgets or artifacts to emerge and operate. Practices which range from the relatively simple and familiar realm of homemaking, cooking, hygiene and the like to the more complex areas of health care, education or defence are all, in a sense, technologies.

From a broad perspective then, a technology can be seen as part and product of a culture.[2] The latter can be understood as the sum total of the material and psychological expressions of a given social group. A culture encompasses a burden of "collective experiences," as ways of doing things, folklore, and other spiritual and/or artistic expressions. Its visible expressions are material: artifacts, utensils, buildings, machines or works of art. Its foundation, however, is language and symbols which could be combined, recombined and modified, making it possible to reproduce and innovate upon the above-mentioned material objects.

A culture is complex, multifaceted and dynamic. In its most abstract sense, *a culture is the software of civilization*. It involves knowledge broadly defined: know-how (technology), know-what, know-why and know-when. The latter three in modern society are synonymous with "science."

In sum, culture comprises the complex gamut of society's reconstruction of reality, from systematic knowledge (philosophy and science), to feelings, morals and intuition. In an Aristotelian way, we can say that a culture includes the collective orientations of all the three aspects of the human mind: a) a praxis (*techné, pratein*), b) the creative knowledge of aesthetics, intuition and inspiration (art and literature, *poiein*) and c) the world of abstract and systematic thought (theory, science, *episteme*).

Technology, Development and Underdevelopment

It is perfectly possible, as has been the case throughout human history, that technological know-how could develop independently from science. In the Western world, the so-called "traditional" or "pre-Newtonian" technologies not only preceded science but often provided the problematic basis for scientific discovery. Invention for problem-solving, as far back as the mid 19th century often came before theoretical reflection and scientific research. This meant that scientifically-based technologies did not become predominant until well into the Industrial Revolution. This separation began to change as a consequence of educational innovations such as Napoleon's creation of the *Polytechnique*. The subsequent application in the 1880s of the newly integrated notion of a scientific and

---

[1] See Bernhard Stern, "Some Aspects of Historical Materialism," in the Sponsoring Committee of the Bernhard J. Stern Memorial Fund, *Historical Sociology: The Selected Papers of Bernhard J. Stern*, (New York: Citadel Press, 1959), pp.15–35.

[2] See Ricardo Israel-Zipper, *Un Mundo Cercano. El Impacto Político y Económico de las Nuevas Tecnologías*, (Santiago: Instituto de Ciencia Polltica, Universidad de Chile, 1984), pp.11–30.

technological education in Wilhemian Germany, Meiji Japan and in the United States, brought science and technology in line with each other.

In this day and age, the capacity to deal with complex problems and to retool know-how, requires a systematic (scientific) understanding of reality. In this sense, we talk about a "scientific" as opposed to a "theological" or "metaphysical" culture. The leading edge of technology is given by research and development (R&D). This relatively novel phenomenon is particularly pronounced in the most industrialized societies. It is here that a phenomenal discontinuity exists between "developed" and "underdeveloped" societies. In the latter, not only the instrumentalities of Western technologies are being transferred but native technologies, with a considerable lineage and time investment, are being truncated by the surreptitious importation of the soft technologies and values which accompany Western hardware.

The "environmental impact" of a technology is not only upon the physical environment. Culture is the most seriously affected yet the least studied. In a sense, via technological innovation, the fundamental values inscribed in the cultural software are being altered and eroded, often leading to a breakdown of civilization. Cultural alienation often results, i.e. having a solution before defining the problem, or worse, trying to adapt the problem to a standard and "pre-packed" solution.

Cultural and technological alienation, nevertheless, are not only a Third World phenomenon. As our inability to relate technologies and technological change to our own lives increases, technological dysfunctions have become daily occurrences in the industrialized West. Somehow, the velocity of change, combined with a *super-specialization enforced by the educational system* and a concomitant tendency to separate ethical-moral questions from "productive rationality" is at the core of such alienation. Undeniably, the *present* association between humans and *their* technologies, and the environment is far from healthy. This raises grave concerns about the future. Technologically-induced crises, including resource depletion, pollution, environmental damage and the spectre of nuclear war threaten global survival, not to mention Humanity's material, political and spiritual quality of life. All these destructive trends are becoming global. The practice of developed regions and peoples to "dump" their waste and growth problems and throw their might upon the "lesser developed" ones has boomeranged. Conventional responses to poverty and human and ecological degradation based upon "more" and easy technical fixes (including military ones), far from providing solutions, compound existing malfunctions. This creates new and deeper crises: *global underdevelopment.*

Technology and Values

What we often forget in doom analysis is that technology is a human product. Technology alters the *physical* world but its *foundations* are in the *"software"* (or *"programming code"*) *of civilization.* In this sense a technology is never, nor can it be, neutral and ideology-free. In fact, it *reflects the power structure of a society* and is *intrinsically political.*[1] This association between technology and values is

---

[1] Israel, *op.cit.,* p.25.

easy to understand in "simpler" or more "primitive" societies. However, it appears blurred to us due to the hegemonic cultural role of "hard" sciences and "positive" economics in our culture.

Technical "know-how" becomes more and more conditioned by a narrow definition of scientific "know-why" and increasingly less concerned with morality, will, responsibility and consequences. Thus, modern technology is dominated by the rationality of specialized and fragmented scientific "truths" and by the short-run economic "bottom line" of cost-benefit. In this, Economics is seen by many as a surrogate morality—or oracle—based upon objective and explicit calculation. The Moral Philosophy of Smith and Ricardo, if deprived of its ethical foundations (i.e. "the Protestant ethic"), far from being a guideline for rational and moral action, becomes a simple justificatory catechism for princes and merchants. Growth becomes an end in itself.

Therefore, *technology does not run out of control; people do.* A few have a vested interest in maintaining the present thrust: they benefit from it, even if the future consequences were to be devastating. Others do so for ideological reasons: the "progressive optimism" which permeates today's scientific and technological discourse. Many, in a sort of technological nihilism, feel that nothing can be done and turn from responsibility or "just don't care." The above technological determinism[1] is a *cultural pathology* based upon the dogmatic belief that only "prudent" and incremental solutions are workable. These piecemeal and narrow approaches, however, only serve to reinforce the status quo. Such pseudo-pragmatism is not an intrinsic component of technology or science. Nor is it rational. The tendency to separate what Karl Mannheim calls "substantive" from "functional" rationality[2] is in fact an *ideological* legacy of the Industrial Revolution applied to a world whose conditions and technical capabilities are radically different from those of the past. While the "separation of science from faith, from ethics and from art"[3] constituted an essential step in the development of modern civilization, nowadays it may well be a cultural directive leading to entropy.[4] Humanity has the ability to overcome and even reverse the current crisis and usher civilization into a New Renaissance. The key for taking control of technology lies also in the cultural

---

[1]
Cf. Barry Jones, *Sleepers, Wake! Technology and the Future of Work*, (Oxford: Oxford University Press, 1982), pp.210–238.

[2]
Cf. Karl Mannheim, *Diagnosis of Our Time. Wartime Essays of a Sociologist*, (London: Routledge and Kegan Paul, 1962), *passim*. Mannheim distinguishes between two types of modern rationalities—substantive and functional. The former refers to a rationality of ends, i.e. the ability of an actor to perceive the circumstances, interrelatedness and consequences of his or her acts. The latter basically entails a rationality of means, i.e. the ability of an actor to apply "know-how" and technique to a problem irrespective of its environmental circumstances or its effects.

[3]
See John U. Nef, *Cultural Foundations of Industrial Civilization*, (New York: Harper and Brothers, 1960), p.4.

[4]
See Wolfgang Koerner, "Rationality and Reaction: The Root of Modernity," in Tom Darby, (Ed.), *Sojourns in the New World. Reflections on Technology*, (Ottawa: Carleton University Press, 1986), pp.183–190.

software: self-correction and adaptation through *learning*. This book is an invitation to expand our collective horizons in the process of learning.

DR. J. NEF is Professor of Political Studies at the University of Guelph.

2 *Fred H. Knelman*

Historical and Contemporary Perspectives of Science, Technology, and Ethics

Technology is a social process of applying the ensemble of technical means and knowledge to serve social ends. Because it is social progress involving actors organized within structures and having roles, goals and values, technology becomes amenable to sociological analysis. In its broadest definition, technology is the totality of technical means employed by a culture for the production and control of material and non-material goods and services. Technology is also embedded in the paradigms of rationality and what is believed to constitute the social good, i.e. the social paradigm of progress. Technology is also the creator of unique and unprecedented environments which yield new patterns of social organization, behaviour and choice and which impact on the natural environment. Because technology is so closely connected to the core of means and ends, it also impacts on the ethical environment.

It is the socialization of technology and its relationship to social change that often escapes the attention of its analysts. Basically, technology encompasses technical practices, products, practitioners and process, institutionally organized and directed towards human and societal goals which may be reduced to profit and power. A further subtlety is that technology is both hardware and software and that it encompasses both the production of tools, instruments and machines, as well as the application of a broad array of techniques, all based on the discoveries of science—physical, biological and social. Thus modern brain-washing and mind-altering techniques, i.e. the mediation of psychological, behavioral and spiritual states are as much a part of technology as computers and missiles, as are genetic engineering, organ transplants, artificial intelligence and test-tube babies.

What must be emphasized is that modern technology differs from the inventions of the past or even the more concentrated and organized products of the Industrial Revolution in at least two fundamental ways. The first is that the modern process of innovation has created a science–technology continuum. The preexisting boundary and time separations between scientific discovery, early application and commercial diffusion has become a single organized related activity. The second is that this process of innovation or research, development and demonstration (R, D and D) has become institutionalized within government, businesses and technology corporations. The result is the acceleration of results, the rapid diffusion of these results and the equally rapid impacts on society. The impacts on the natural environment may also be rapid but often the more insidious are delayed due to the relative size and resilience of the impactor and the impacted ecosystem. However, the exponential increase in rate, scale and magnitude of technological interventions have approached a level of real threat to the global ecosystem, viz.

the nuclear winter of our discontent. Not only have the tools of innovation become far more powerful, but the resources—physical, financial and human—have also become far more powerful and far more organized. This is the socialization of technology, quite distinct from pre-science, the inventions. What must be emphasized is that there now exists a science-technology continuum in which research, development, demonstration and commercial/social application are organizationally linked.

While creativity was a common factor in invention and innovation, the former was more the product of ingenuity and stubborn persistence and sometimes, as in the case of Marconi's wireless telegraphy, the source of new science. A further distinction is that invention focussed on extensions of muscle power while the development of instruments that extended human senses came largely in the post-scientific period and were necessary for the evolution of experimental science, leading to the discovery of the laws of matter and motion. Chemistry lagged behind physics due in large part to the inhibiting influence of Aristotelian views of material change. Nuclear physics and microbiology were even more dependent on the development of sophisticated instruments. When inventions preceded the social environment required for their use, they were viewed as toys. This was true of Hero of Alexandria who invented the steam engine in an age of slavery.

While our definition of technology may appear all-embracing technology is only one sub-system in a social system comprising several other key sub-systems, i.e. economics, politics and culture, all of which interact and are connected through information flows and feed-back mechanisms. These sub-systems are defined by having identifiable boundaries, internal dynamics, as well as structural and organizational coherence. It is through these characteristics that we can separate and distinguish the technology sub-system. An analysis of the relationships of technology with the other social sub-systems and the total system is essential to our understanding.

Technology in History

The very oldest tools were the hone pebbles discovered by Robert Leakey at East Rudolf in northern Kenya in 1969 and carbon-dated at 2,600,000 years old. Fire was mastered by Peking Man about 350,000 years ago at the end of the Second Ice Age. With the arrival of Modern Man or homo sapiens in Europe some 10,000 years ago, we saw the development of fish hooks, needles, spears, bows, blow pipes, bolas and primitive art. After the end of the last Ice Age, the major invention was agriculture and its complements, followed by fabrics, spinning and weaving, which began and later flourished in Egypt between 4000 and 6500 years ago. The first Bronze Age civilization was that of the Shang Dynasty, founded about 1750 B.C. Chinese metal working was by far the most advanced of its time. By the 5th century B.C., they were smelting iron, copper, tin, silver and lead. They grew millet and rice and cultivated the silkworm to produce fine fabrics. They had invented the abacus for calculation, and, by 200 B.C., the crossbow which was the most important development in armaments. By the 11th century, they had invented a sophisticated version of gunpowder, earlier known in Europe as "Greek fire."

It is not possible to do justice to the contributions to science and technology of each historical civilization and empire that rose to power. But contributions to certified knowledge and major inventions were made by Chinese, Egyptian, Minoan, Moslem, Roman and Greek ages. Technical development, which we now associate almost completely with Western civilization, was the product of these earlier periods and, in fact, much of what had been known was temporarily lost in the upheavals that followed the decline and fall of the Roman Empire. Slowly in the Middle Ages, the arts of technology were reintroduced into the West. The glory of the Middle Ages was undeniably architecture, the Gothic cathedral and its exquisite arches, vaults and spires and, of course, the artistry of stained glass. Immediately following the Middle Ages was the age of exploration and discovery, based on the new navigational instruments and the design of the great sailing ships.

The greatest discovery was in the realm of ideas made by the Greek natural philosophers, beginning in the 3rd century B.C. They were the first to seek natural explanations of the natural world and through the use of deductive reasoning, to develop generalized theories of natural phenomena. The influence of Plato and Aristotle persisted through the Middle Ages.

The Scientific Revolution

In the two and a half centuries between 1473 and 1727, the greatest intellectual revolution in human history occurred—the Scientific Revolution—initiated by the work of a relatively small group of geniuses working in the universities of Western Europe such as Paris, Bologna, Padua, Oxford and Cambridge. This development rested on social circumstance as well as critical invention. Certainly the invention of printing with moveable type about 1450 by Johann Gutenberg in the German city of Mainz permitted the necessary communication of ideas and experiments. At the same time, the voyages of discovery spawned navigation-based empires of trade and conquest in the 15th and 16th centuries. The language of science, mathematics, was born with the invention of logarithms by Napier, with algebra and descriptive geometry of Descartes in the late 16th century, and with calculus by Leibniz and Newton in the latter half of the 17th century. At the same time, the most powerful tool of all, scientific method, evolved with Bacon and Descartes and climaxed with Galileo. The discovery of new worlds of geography and scientific principles were born together, creating a new world view, eventually to become the basis of a new world order. Scientific research became institutionalized. Science became recognized as a profession with the creation of scientific academies in Italy, England and France in the 17th century. The British Royal Society was created by Charles II in 1662 and is today the most prestigious of all academies. From the beginning, its charter explicitly recognized the value of science for the state, particularly the mastery of navigation, the basis of the British Empire. Scientific journals appeared at this time, greatly contributing to the dissemination and spread of science. But Francis Bacon's utopian vision of science in the service of the state, described in his *New Atlantis*, was not to be realized. Physics flourished as the laws of mechanics, motion, light, gravity and medicine were discovered. As we have indicated earlier, chemistry lagged behind mechanics

and began, in large part, with the publishing of Lavoisier's *Elementary Treatise on Chemistry* in 1789.

The French Revolution

The marriage of knowledge and the state began early in history with the special status of soothsayers and savants. But the works of these early advisors to the Prince were limited in application. While it is true that Archimedes' and Galileo's military inventions were useful, they were not in the mainstream of their life work, i.e. geometry and physics. But after science came of age, the scientist became "a truthful magician, a daemon of the positive" as Bachelard so poetically puts it—and we might add, not merely of the positive but of the possible.

It was the revolutionary committee of the French Republic that first clearly laid claim to science as the servant of the state. This period also saw the creation of the first institute of higher education devoted to technology, the *Ecole Polytechnique*, which became a model for applied science and engineering schools. It was designed to train engineers and army officers who were the predecessors of technologists. The French Revolution produced a messianic vision of the role of science in the age of Enlightenment.

The most utopian vision of the role of science in the Age of Enlightenment was expressed by the philosopher of the French Revolution, the Marquis de Condorcet. In his book, *Fragment sur L'Atlantide*, he writes about the tenth or final stage of human history, in effect a universal republic of science which would couple the climax of scientific rationality with the triumph of democracy. In this empire of reason, science would remove both superstition and inequality. In Condorcet's naive model of the republic of science, it would be the state which would have the major function of supporting the republic of science for the progress of society. It was the French Revolution that enlisted scientists in the cause of the revolution.

The Industrial Revolution

Later philosophers of science, such as August Comte, believed that the Industrial Revolution would create a new priesthood of scientists whose religion was reason, and while pursuing pure truth, would nevertheless guard the moral imperatives while industrialists and bankers, concerned with production and growth, would replace warriors, thus creating an age of peace. Yet, despite impassioned pleas for state support of science and scientists, such as that of Charles Babbage in England and Renan and Pasteur in France, it was industry, not the state, that first aided research. This was not basic research, but research much more concerned with the work of technologists in factory applications. The Industrial Revolution, which created the first industrial factory production system, was not primed by science but by invention which often spawned science. James Watt first improved the steam engine in 1765. Some 37 years later, it was perfected with the development of high pressure steam and the age of the railroad began. But the laws of thermodynamics took another 25 years to be discovered.

Governments did not comprehend the close link between the support of science and the furthering of economic and political power. All through the Industrial Revolution of the 19th century there was a general lag of some 35 years or more between scientific discovery and commercial application, i.e. between the discovery of electromagnetic induction and industrial dynamos; and between benzene chemistry and the commercial production of dye stuffs. This was equally true for all the major scientific discoveries, i.e. the electron, Thomson in 1897; radium, Curie in 1898; special relativity, Einstein in 1905. Their technological application was witnessed in the atom bomb in 1945.

In summary, utopian visions of a republic of science as expressed by Francis Bacon in the *New Atlantis* (1627) i.e. "The end of our foundation is the knowledge of causes and secret motions and things; and the enlarging of the bounds of human empire, to the effecting of all things possible" become the dystopia of industrial pollution and weapons of mass destruction. Technology quickly assumed its dynamic laissez-faire character in which "all things possible" included the good, the bad and the ugly. As Amory Lovins describes it, "What is not specifically forbidden becomes compulsory"—and very little is forbidden and often too little and too late. However, while industrial technology was employed in the period of World War I, it was not until the World War II that the marriage of science/technology and the state was consummated with some preliminary wooing during the depression years under Roosevelt's New Deal, and in France, under the Popular Front. In the latter case, the first science minister was appointed in 1935. Actually, the most direct claim on science to serve the state occurred in Soviet Russia and Nazi Germany although subservient to the rigid orthodoxies of their relative ideologies, which inhibited scientific expansion. Interestingly, it was the Nazi threat that led to the ultimate expression of Big Science, the "Manhattan Project," which became the model of technological development. And the future was to provide the technologists with a source of power and privilege as industry, government and universities vied for their favours.

Technology and Society: The Technological Order

The technological order is a sociological model of technology in Western urbanized industrialized societies. Its basic characteristics are the dominance of science and technology over the economics, politics and culture of these societies—the relative autonomy of technological growth—acting outside both the natural world and rational human choice. An equally significant aspect of the technological order is the exponential growth rate of all areas of science and technology. Given this phenomenal growth and the irresistible rewards in terms of political and economic power for technological eminence, technology tends to be anti-ecological in operation and in values.

The consequences of the technological order and the inevitable cultural lags between the growth of technology and the growth of social and belief systems to control and use if for human welfare has created a world crisis in values. An inevitable backlash also occurs in the form of the largely unprecedented and unassessed hazards of technology. Pollution in all its forms is the prime example of this backlash having brought us to a global environmental crisis. An inevitable backlash also occurs in the form of the largely unprecedented and unassessed hazards of technology. Pollution in all its forms is the prime example of this backlash having brought us to a global environmental crisis.

One of the most complete and compelling technological models is the work of the French sociologist, Jacques Ellul.[1] According to Ellul's idea, technology results in complete human subversion through the accumulation and supremacy of techniques, that is, of means over ends. Man becomes the victim of technique. This is the price we pay for both progress and survival. His model does not allow for the intervention of human will or choice, the renunciation of technology or the possibility of social control. It is a totally determinist theory viewing technology as the complete ensemble of techniques, of tools, tool-making and programs to modify and manipulate the physical, biological, psychological and social environment. It rests on a concept that "manipulative rationality" is omniscient.

At the outset, we reject technological determinism as we reject the complete renunciation of technology. We believe there can be technology without tears as we believe we need technology to survive. But these attributes require a radical revision in the social relations of technology and in the social structure that must command it.

A strange correspondence on this issue of technological optimism is that the economically developed world, communist and non-communist, share a common faith in science and technology. For each, science and technology are automatically transformed into servants of the people, human welfare and fulfillment. Thus, the Russian and American new technocrats speak with a single tongue—the ideology of progress transcending the differences in political philosophy.

In all technological phenomena, there is a clear tendency for technological traffic to outpace technological control and regulatory systems. The unique phenomena of "rate and magnitude problems" are an inherent aspect of the vast increase in technological traffic. This is true for chemicals, automobiles, weapons and nuclear fuel cycles. Moreover, the rising costs of control and regulations erode the fictitious economic advantages of many of these technologies. The economic order cannot maintain itself with an uncontrolled system which only leads to disorder. This is the systemic failure of the entire economic system. Deficit and deferred budgeting reinforced by large social subsidies has created a heritage of false accounting in which new costs of growth continue to appear and accumulate in the future. Environmentally induced disease is a prime example of the present system, but so is the vast increase in psychosocial pathology, crimes without motivation in the more existential manifestation of violence. Both structural and unstructured violence are accelerating.

Today we can identify some of those problems whose scope and urgency threaten the survival of civilization. To some degree, we can even quantify the path of their development but as yet cannot predict accurately the timing of disaster. There are four most urgent problems in the world; but as we do not as yet have solutions, they remain dilemmas—energy/resources, equity/distribution, environment and population with its special aspect of food and urbanization. These are not unrelated, but intimately connected. They all represent "Malthusian" dilemmas lodged in uncontrolled and unlimited growth. Due to the lag of the necessary mechanisms of social control, both as institutions and belief systems, these dilemmas will inevitably lead to disaster. They are the "bombs" (P. Ehrlich),

---

[1] Jacques Ellul, *The Technological Society*, (New York: Vintage Books, 1964), *passim.*

"crashes" (G. Rattray Taylor) and "traps" (K. Boulding) leading to population explosions, ecological Armageddon, energy and resource wars or wars of redistribution as the have-nots fight for their share to survive. And the ultimate threat is that war becomes nuclear war. Maldistribution of consumption means maldistribution of health, wealth and justice. It exists within nations and between nations. The new communications have created the "global village" of McLuhan in the sense of instant distribution of information and rising expectancies. But expectancy has risen much faster than fulfillment and the reality of the maldistribution of consumption between economically developed nations and the developing world is such that the vast majority of people in the world can never consume at the US's or Japan's present level. They can never even catch up. Increasing the current tensions is the fact that resources are not distributed in the earth's crust in accordance to the distribution of economic power, the cases of oil and uranium being the most prominent.

Trend Has Become Destiny: Paradigms and Progress

Thomas Kuhn, in his great work, *The Structure of Scientific Revolutions*, used the term, "dominant paradigm" to signify entire sets of unquestioned assumptions, perceptions and ways of thinking about reality. It not only imposes a world view on society and all who share it but excludes certain questions or anomalies as meaningless. It tends to influence a total culture. The "industrial growth—progress—high technology" dominant paradigm is now beset by anomalies, dilemmas, paradoxes and contradictions which it can no longer ignore or cast off. These multiple and irreconcilable dilemmas are intensified by the new scarcity hitting a society based on the assumption of endless plenty. And, perhaps, more importantly, a new plenty of environmental degradation has inflicted a deep wound on the system. The world is ripe for a *paradigm shift*—a new vision which resolves these anomalies.

Modern industrialized societies are obsessed with growth. The historical trend of high growth which emerged in the post World War II period has now been sanctified as manifest destiny.

It is not the counterintuitive nature of industrialized social systems which accounts for their current incapacity to cope with continuous crises, but rather the power of the dominant paradigm which infuses and pervades the policy feedback mechanisms. In terms of "informediation" the *Limits to Growth Study* was characterized as an example of MIMO (Malthus In—Malthus Out). The universal law which governs the policy system is PIPO (Paradigm in—Paradigm Out). Its major characteristic is a basic violation of the very principle of cybernetics, i.e. regulation and control. Feedback tends to be exclusively positive. The message is continued growth and the maximization of the rate of return on all investments whether profit or power. While strong positive feedback places a premium on time, weak negative signals are subject to the general tendency to discount the future. Technology, culture, economics and politics—the major subsystems of our cultural system—are locked into the growth imperative. The imperative becomes intrinsic, even categorical. The net effect is that the system is effectively blind, suffering from exponential myopia. It becomes insensitive to negative feedback signals derived from the mounting environmental and social costs of growth.

Maximization and insensitivity of growth lead to the acceleration of "crashes"—technological, social and environmental. They also lead to new levels of overkill and overskill and the incapacity to timely response. The model of the system becomes the Titanic. To develop or not to develop is never the question.

At the same time, the powerful belief in an "omniscient rationality," linear and reductionist in mode and infused by a technological paradigm of infallibility, continues. In such a social system, trend becomes destiny, the future tends to be extrapolated and the role of experts is to comply and accommodate, as the necessary certification of knowledge is purchased by the political economy. Quantity consistently overcomes quality. In doing so, it first excludes, then denies the qualifiable.

It is not surprising that the very analytic tools which evolve within this system are themselves sensitive to the influence of the dominant paradigm. The quantification imperative is manifest in the techniques of cost/risk—benefit analysis, inflation impact analysis, the notion of "acceptable risk," etc. The effect is that the employed methodologies eliminate the qualification. Elimination is often followed by denial of their value or even existence. That which cannot be measured cannot be meaningful or meaningfully utilized. The legal/regulatory system is also amenable to the penetration of the dominant paradigm. Burden of proof and guilt is placed on the victims of technology while the perpetrators get the benefit of doubt and profit. Thus this present ascendancy of quantity over quality is at once an expression of the current scientific mode of knowing and the paradigmatic influence of the economic imperative. The future is effectively mortgaged and foreclosed.

It thus follows that environmental protection becomes essentially a pseudo-feedback process. Its purpose is political cosmetics. Social goal-seeking becomes self-fulfilling when the institutions designed to develop policy act under a pardigmatic injunction. While it is true that "information precedes compulsion," even the information is compelled. As Karl Deutsch puts its, "A society or community that is to steer itself must continue to receive a full flow of three kinds of information: first, information about the world outside; second, information about the past; and third, information about itself and its own parts. Let any of these three streams be long interrupted ... and the society becomes a walking corpse."[1]

Sociological Analysis of Technological Change

Every invention consists of a new combination of invented elements. Thus an automobile is a carriage plus an internal combustion system plus a transmission. An aeroplane is a combination of a box-kite, a windmill and an internal combustion engine. But inventions are not merely the new combination of existing elements, but also incorporate principles, ideas and scientific discovery. Galileo's telescope, for example, was not merely a combination of lenses set in a cylinder, but also the application of the law of optics. Thus the elements of invention are both material and intellectual.

---

[1]   Karl W. Deutsch, *The Nerves of Government*, (New York: The Free Press, 1966), p.129.

The acceleration of technological growth and of its impacted social and environmental systems is dependent on certain critical factors. These are: 1) the number of existing elements of invention and ideas; 2) the rate of communication of knowledge and the availability of these elements to the inventors; 3) the availability of the necessary physical, human and financial resources; and 4) the existence of organized bodies of research and development.

The invention of the automobile spawned a web of new inventions—highways, road accommodation, service stations, highway police, shopping centres, drive-in theatres and tellers, truck commerce, RV vehicles, auto racing, suburban development, air pollution, automobile insurance, traffic jams, auto accidents and then numerous military applications as well. What one may discern is a web of developments derived from the original mode of the automobile which spawned an industrial complex and spurred new industries such as the oil industry, the auto production industry, the auto service industry, the auto sales industry, used car lots and the demand for a variety of materials from steel to plastics.

The traffic-controls gap has led society to create special institutions and regulations specifically dedicated to these tasks, such as the control and regulation of food and drugs, environmental protection, nuclear regulation, product integrity, arms control and finally, a few brave but until now futile attempts at preventative rather than reactive methods of control. There are social, environmental and technology impact assessment, risk assessment, cost-risk benefit analyses etc. But problems of politics and methodology restrict effectiveness. For one thing, these approaches are responsive rather than anticipatory. For another, problems are reduced to economic measurables effectively eliminating values. A third problem is the inability to increase or maximize returns. Finally, the regulatory bodies are infected with a reluctance to impede growth.

Of all the examples that tend to support the concept of an autonomous technology, none is more compelling than the current operationalized nuclear arsenals of the superpowers. As the warning systems of these major protagonists become increasingly computerized and sensitive to each other, there is an increasing number of ways whereby interacting false alerts could trigger a war. The problem is that the premium on time has led us to create surrogate decision-makers, i.e. computers, and to initiate Launch on Warning (LOW) systems. While we have maintained dual and redundant warning devices, i.e. radars and satellites, the fear of short-warning attacks on nuclear systems coupled to the possibility of common mode failure of redundant systems in a time of greatly enhanced tension, could well lead to the decision to launch through a single unresolved alert. Given the hair trigger state of the confronting arsenals, several catalytic inductions of nuclear war could lead to a nuclear holocaust. In effect, we have created a doomsday machine and rendered the decision to unleash to machines. This is the essence of the Ellulian nightmare.

The Crisis in Values

The ultimate questions raised so far are those of human values. This period is one of transition: traditional values, unable to serve survival or fulfillment, are being shattered by the acceleration of social change, and a new code, while generally viewed as necessary, is not yet clearly defined or operational. Moreover, the source of this value crisis seems to be contemporary technology with its necessary dichotomies of power and love, growth and control, quantity and quality, profit and welfare. The pervasive nature of technology finally creates a technological environment in which all our needs, basic and otherwise, are themselves the products of technology. Food, clothing, buildings, cities and media become technologized and, in so doing, alienated from the natural world. Nature becomes the target of endless technological alteration and manipulation, coupled to a myopia of consequences, including the myopia of exponential growth. We have invented multiple means to our own end.

The systems of the value crisis are everywhere. Stress, alienation, and disorientation take their toll on man's psychosocial balance. New disquietude threatens us every day. The war is not confined to Africa or Central America or the Middle East. It is in our streets, in our homes, and in ourselves. Affluence and poverty confront each other between citizens and nations. The human rights gap transcends all boundaries of culture and ideology and entrenched authority is being challenged everywhere from the home to government.

All the problems of uncontrolled growth that we discussed previously are ultimately questions of human values. They all involve a crisis of choice. This is the decade of ultimate choice. Unless we can discover the solutions we will perish. The solutions involve a change in our values and a revolutionary restructuring of our national and international economic and political systems. Fortunately, the explosion in science and technology is now being matched by an explosion of human consciousness and conscience—a revolution of hope. People everywhere in the world are beginning to stir. The material hang-up, with its growth syndrome and power complex, is being questioned in fundamental terms. Scientists and technologists are central figures in this crisis. They are adopting an operational ethic involving relevance and responsibility and assuming the role of an early warning system. They are beginning to adopt a new professional ethic of assessment and concern. Young engineers are questioning their professional training and practices, demanding a more interdisciplinary approach and, in particular, an ecological concern for their products and processes. Also, an operational ethic, "When in ignorance, refrain" is being adopted by some of the younger technologists. Scientists and engineers are beginning to think in terms of a "technology of cure" and a "technology of assessment and control." Some have proposed the mobilization of large-scale, even worldwide, groups of creative thinkers to work toward the resolution of our crises. In sum, many are holding out the hope that participation in government may assure the retention of human values, of diversity and unity, freedom and responsibility. Only hope, commitment, and involvement have survival value and can bring the dominant paradigm into its proper perspective.

DR. F.H. KNELMAN is a teacher, writer, and peace activist. He won the White Owl Conservation Award as Canada's outstanding environmentalist in 1972. He currently serves on the Peace Committee, Vancouver City Council.

3   *Julia Schtivelman / Hugh C. Russell*

Sustainable Development, Human Resources, and Technology

Environmentally sound development is urgently needed in both the North and the South. With the publication of the Brundtland Commission Report on the environment and development, *Our Common Future*, the concept of sustainable development has come to play a prominent role in the development dialogue. The concept of sustainable development, a harmonious coexistence of economic growth with a renewed and vigorous emphasis on environmental sensitivity is a tantalizing one. INCO, one of the "dirty dozen," has already invested $500,000 in new furnaces that have the capacity to reduce sulphur dioxide emissions.[1]

The challenge for business worldwide is to rise to the occasion of sustainable development. However, there is an even greater challenge for the rest of the world. Sustainable development is not just another development buzzword. It relates as much to the industrialized countries of the North as it does to the Third World. Japan, for example, has emerged as a leader among industrialized nations in the production and export of environmentally clean technologies.[2]

After the Japanese environmental crisis of the 1960s, government regulations and response to the victims of environmentally spawned diseases (Minamata disease being the most famous) have resulted in innovative approaches by Japanese industry to limit pollution and still maintain Japan's staggering economic growth.[3] Presently, producers of "clean" technology in Japan are the stars of the stock market. Japan's record in exporting environmentally hazardous industry to its periphery, especially to Indonesia and Ireland, is certainly not perfect. However, within national boundaries, Japan provides a good example of environmentalism with growth.[4]

But, we must realize that no amount of "clean" technologies will further the goals of sustainable development unless the root cause of environmental degra-

---

[1] Robert Collison, "The Greening of the Boardroom" in *Report on Business Magazine*, (July 1989), p.44.

[2] Steven Reed, "Environmental Politics: Some Reflections based on the Japanese Case." *Comparative Politics*, Vol. 13, No. 3., (1981).

[3] Norie Huddle and Michael Reich, *Island of Dreams: Environmental Crisis in Japan*, (Cambridge Mass.: Schenkman Books Inc., 1987).

[4] Adam Meyerson, "Japan: Environmentalism with Growth," *The Washington Post*, (September 5, 1980).

dation and resource depletion is addressed directly and swiftly. In the industrialized world, the greatest threat to the environment is consumerism, whereas in the developing world, poverty is nature's worst enemy.

Poverty pushes the small-scale farmer to exhaust already marginal soils, over-fish waters, and continually clear forested areas for fuel wood and agricultural production. Poverty forces women to walk for miles in search of wood and water. Poverty causes people to put survival ahead of environmental protection. Indeed poverty forces people into a vicious circle where environmental degradation leads to poverty and poverty causes environmental degradation.

Moreover, at the national level, a developing county with a high international debt cannot afford to preserve forests at the expense of the survival of the people. Edward Goldsmith and Nicholas Hildyard report that since 1982, the Third World has received less money in aid from the industrialized countries than it has paid out in interest on loans. In 1986 this negative transfer amounted to US$29 million.[1] The enormity of the environmental and social costs of the debt crisis cannot be overestimated or overlooked.

Sustainable development has an essentially normative character, which makes it difficult to operationalize. It implies a close relationship between environmental sensitivity and economic growth. Within sustainable development, economic and social objectives are balanced against nature's constraints. A spirit of solidarity with future generations is included in the concept. Sustainable development is based upon the familiar principles of self reliance, fulfillment of basic needs and an emphasis on the quality of life. It requires:

- Harmonization of consumption patterns, time use and life styles
- Appropriate technologies, ecologically-based designs
- Low energy profile, promotion of renewable energy base
- New uses for environmental resources
- Careful husbandry of resources, recycling
- Ecological principles to guide settlement patterns and land uses
- Participatory planning and grass-roots activation.[2]

The greatest underutilized natural and renewable resources of the earth are humans. Sustainable development emphasizes a harmony of economics and the environment, suggesting that environmental sensitivity makes good business sense. The Brundtland World Commission on the environment and development states that without environmental preservation there can be no economic growth, and conversely, in the absence of a robust economy, environmental considerations are given low priority in development projects. The Brundtland Commission also argues that

---

[1]

Edward Goldsmith and Nicholas Hildyard, (eds.), *The Earth Report: The Essential Guide to Global Ecological Issues*, (Los Angeles: Price Stern Sloan, Inc., 1988), pp.219–220.

[2]

United Nations Centre on Transnational Corporations, *Environmental Aspects of the Activities of Transnational Corporations: A Survey*, (New York, 1985), pp.2–3

human resource development is a crucial requirement not only to build up technical knowledge and capabilities, but also to create new values to help individuals and nations cope with rapidly changing social, environmental, and development realities. Knowledge shared globally would assure greater mutual understanding and create willingness to share global resources equitably.[1]

Human resource development (HRD), in the context of sustainable development, has special meanings. The bottom-line is *learning*, i.e., an individualized process whereby people fulfill their needs through the internalization of information and the externalization of reactions to environmental conditions. The contexts for such involvement in development include political, socio-cultural, economic and technical-scientific activities. The goals of human resource development in the context of sustainable development include an increased awareness and responsibility for environmental preservation (attitude change), strengthening organizations or developing new ones to deal with environmental issues (organization development), creation, analysis and dissemination of information on the environment (data bases and information), decisions and actions based on information (planning and management), and acquisition of income generating skills in harmony with environmental preservation (employment).

In order to operationalize sustainable development, developing countries must have access to state of the art environmental technology. One of the means available to bridge the widening technological gap between the North and the South is education and training. HRD in sustainable development yields:

- Support for the creation of independent learning about the environment and how to interact with it
- Strengthening of indigenous efficacy in development activities and environmental preservation
- Reinforcement for changes in attitudes about the environment
- Skills to adapt to changing needs as society responds to environmental crises
- Replicability of HRD without external inputs

HRD for sustainable development must also focus on the role of women. There is a direct link between women in developing countries and the use that is made of forests, fields and water. Most small scale farmers in developing countries are women. Programmes which give women greater control over their lives contribute to environmental and overall development sustainability.

Look, for example, at the relationship between resource utilization and income-generating skill for women. Population growth puts pressure on a society to clear the land for food production. Hence, one way to alleviate such pressures is to lower population growth. Indicators which correlate most closely with fertility decline are the education and employment of women, and reductions in infant mortality. Basic literacy training, skills development for income-generation and improved

---

1

World Commission on Environment and Development, *Our Common Future*, (Oxford: The University Press, 1987).

primary health care services—all focused on women—will reduce population growth rates, thereby alleviating pressures on food production, deforestation and other forms of unsustainable resource utilization.[1]

The classic image of a farmer learning about and successfully applying an appropriate technology is an example of sustainability and HRD. Initially, the result is enhanced productivity, but the farmer also learns of the long-term benefits of environmental sensitivity. Acquired technology coupled with ecologically sound agricultural techniques is environmentalism with growth.[2]

At the local level, community development projects, citizens' movements, non-governmental organizations (NGOs)[3], private sector organizations and government training and credit institutions have a direct impact on development needs. Here, organizational development, institution-building and other HRD activities are necessary to strengthen indigenous capacities to alleviate poverty and increase equity in society. Community participation from the planning and decision-making phases to project execution, is a prerequisite for sustainable development.[4] The user must be empowered with the control and the responsibility for the use of the resource.[5]

Successful local organizations are at the front line of sustainable development in that they

- provide two-way flows of technical information that supports those individuals trying new methods
- break down barriers between groups and individuals
- reduce risk to a minimum
- adapt project activities to local conditions
- marshal local resources
- achieve greater political and economic independence for local people by exercising influence over locally based administration and presenting claims to government
- coordinate and spread the benefits of outside assistance.

---

[1]

Lester R. *Brown, et al., State of the World,* A Worldwatch Institute Report on Progress toward a Sustainable Society, (New York: 1988).

[2]

George Honadale and Jerry VanSant, *Implementation for Sustainability: Lessons from Integrated Rural Development*, (Connecticut: Kumarian Press, 1985).

[3]

Non-government organizations are non-profit organizations; as such they neither represent government nor private (for profit) sectors. In developing countries, they are usually community-based organizations dedicated to economic and social development activities.

[4]

Arthur J. Hanson, "Sustainable Development in Indonesia" in *Pearsonnotes*, Volume 4, Number 2, (Spring 1989), Dalhousie University.

[5]

Madeline Smout, "Community Forestry in Nepal" in *Pearsonnotes*, Volume 4, Number 2, (Spring 1989), p.4, Dalhousie University.

At this stage of implementation HRD is particularly useful because if people are trained to value and respect the environment and to implement environmentally sustainable projects, the result is sustainable livelihoods.

At the regional level, the focus of HRD is on integrated regional development planning, ecological profiling, land use planning, facilitating environment sector reviews and conducting sector studies. At the project level, HRD is useful in environmental impact assessment, rapid assessment studies and the provision of environmental guidelines.[1]

At the national level, policy-makers have the responsibility to provide a mandate, structure and resource framework for sustainable development. Major economic and social changes are going to be required for sustainable development to succeed. Land reform, income redistribution, rationalization of public ownership of businesses and other equity and market reforms are essential. HRD interventions are needed to increase government policy-makers', planners' and sectoral managers' awareness of their responsibilities for environmental preservation, and to facilitate their skills acquisition in policy-making and program planning. Management know-how is critical for sustainable development.

At this level one of the most significant contributors to problems of waste and resource utilization is the rural-urban drift confronting most LDC's (least developing countries). Rapid urbanization causes serious environmental damage in urban and rural areas alike. Therefore policy-makers have to become aware of the ramifications of development policies on the demographics of their countries. They need to learn how to plan development in a manner which ensures manageable demographic shifts. For example, new project analysis of the economics of scale can lead to support for small decentralized and disbursed enterprises which can relieve pressures of urbanization. HRD at the national level includes the development of country environmental profiles, national conservation strategies and country strategy studies.[2] It is at the state level that vertical programs must be integrated in a broad development framework for sustainable development.

At the international level donor agencies have the opportunity to influence improved environmental husbandry in the Third World through the judicious support of sustainable projects. Projects should be evaluated based on their compatibility with sustainable development internationally. HRD must also be harnessed in the implementation process. Donor agencies should harmonize the skills of delivery within their own staff and, through international cooperation, with counterparts in developing countries.

HRD has an additional role at the international level. HRD specialists are needed to help mount global campaigns to foster public support and political will in order to influence people in industrialized countries to manage their own resources and wastes more responsibly. Political will is essential because it must be present for the successful implementation of sustainable projects. Maintaining infrastructure,

---

[1] Czech Conroy, and Miles Litvinoff, eds. *The Greening of Aid: Sustainable Livelihoods in Practice*, (London: Earthscan Publications, 1988).

[2] *Ibid.*

adopting appropriate technologies, providing resources and empowering sub-national bodies, all reflect political priorities.[1] HRD strategies must be used for awareness-building to prepare public opinion in industrialized nations for the changes of life style that will accompany sustainable practices. They will also be necessary to build institutions and technical skills necessary to solve the problems associated with waste reduction and disposal.

The changes which are sought in the process of development are uncertain and complex. Since individuals cannot induce these changes singlehandedly, organizations, project management units, line ministries, political parties, cooperatives, formal village associations, informal seasonal agricultural work groups, and national governments are all examples of target groups for environmentally sustainable development education.[2]

The greatest impact on environmental security can be achieved by mounting HRD and other programs which effectively reduce hunger, increase employment, stem the tide of disease, stimulate equity in social and economic sectors and provide a social, economic and political environment in which problems of governance and international cooperation can be creatively resolved. Human resource development may hold the key to environmentally sustainable development technology.

These are only a few of the priority applications of HRD to the goals of sustainable development. In sum, human institutions have to be matched to ecological realities if humanity is to learn to reverse the disastrous fragmentation of the planet's ecosystems. The fragmentation does not discriminate between LDC's and developed countries. It pervades all countries and peoples of the earth. HRD encompasses a variety of methodologies which are useful for influencing the nature and direction of human institutions. As such it is a vital resource for sustainable development.

At present, the human life style can be defined as ego-systemic. Our answer to organic waste is holding our nose. We deny acid rain, ignore the greenhouse effect, and cut more roads through cities to alleviate traffic congestion. Our attitude to nature is exploitative and domineering and our view of the future is egocentric. Those who dismiss *Our Common Future* as yet another in the series of doomsday texts prefer to avoid the contemporary realities of human survival. An alternative ecosystemic approach is needed. To infectious diseases the response should be disease prevention and health promotion. Alternative energy sources should be sought to alleviate the problem of acid rain. An emergent adaptive and evolving

---

[1]
Ibid.

[2]
Honadle and VanSant, *op. cit.*

view of the future must prevail. In this quest, human resource development is a base for a sustainable future.

HUGH C. RUSSELL is Associate Director, Foundation for International Training (FIT), Toronto.
JULIA SCHTIVELMAN is Special Assistant for Sustainable Development at the Foundation for International Training (FIT), Toronto.[1]

This is a condensed version of a paper entitled, Human Resources for Sustainable Development. Copies may be obtained by writing to: Julia Schtivelman, Foundation for International Training, 1262 Don Mills Road, Suite 200, Don Mills, Ontario, Canada M3B 2W7.

---

[1] FIT is an international non-governmental non-profit organization committed to human resource development in the Third World. Since its inception in 1978, FIT has successfully completed over 250 projects in 40 developing countries. FIT's capabilities are drawn from an international roster of consultants. FIT's projects include community and institution building, technical support to local NGOs, management training, skills development and microenterprise development. FIT is supported by the Canadian International Development Agency (CIDA) and other donors.

4
Paul T. Durbin

Examining the Record: A Bibliographical Note

As editor of the publications of the Society for Philosophy and Technology for the past fifteen years, I have been in contact with philosophers of technology, as well as with historians, social scientists, and scientists, engineers, and physicians throughout the world interested in science, technology, medicine, and social values. My personal concerns are not primarily with ethical or moral choices of individuals. I am especially interested in the social and institutional responsibilities of the scientific, technological, and biomedical communities; and even more particularly in how these responsibilities are being met.

But I find much more interesting and challenging a set of urgent social problems linked to technology. Technological innovation and development, despite its many advantages, can also present problems that range from issues of survival (e.g., the nuclear arms race, nuclear and other toxic wastes and threats to the global ecology) to major issues affecting the quality of life—from inequities between the technologically rich and the poor, to problems associated with technological workplaces, to problems of urban blight and alienation resulting from high-technology development, to problems of privacy as threatened by electronic gadgetry, as well as problems in education, the media, and commercialized "high culture."

These issues are well-known. What we need, however, rather than a further elaboration of the problems, are responses and solutions.

Claims about the Social Responsibilities of Scientists, Engineers and Health Practitioners and Researchers

The claim that scientists have "special" social responsibilities first reached a significant audience in the United States in the aftermath of the US's dropping of atomic bombs on Hiroshima and Nagasaki at the end of World War II. This response was institutionalized in a number of American publications.[1]

This particular claim has continued to be made ever since. In 1975, the Committee on Scientific Freedom and Responsibility of the American Association

---

[1] *The Bulletin of the Atomic Scientists* (see Len Ackland and Steven McGuire, eds., *Assessing the Nuclear Age* [1986], and Morton Grodzins and Eugene Rabinowitch, eds., *The Atomic Age* [1963]—both collections of articles from the *Bulletin*) and the Pugwash movement (see Joseph Rotblat, *Scientists in Quest for Peace: A History of the Pugwash Conferences* [1972]).

for the Advancement of Science issued a report, *Scientific Freedom and Respon-sibility*, in which the claim was repeated in a quasi-official form.

In 1980, AAAS published a set of proceedings, *AAAS* Professional Ethics Project: Professional Ethics Activities in the Scientific and Engineering Societies[1]. The document begins with: "This final report of the AAAS Professional Ethics Project, prepared by the office of the AAAS Committee on Scientific Freedom and Responsibility, builds upon a long-standing concern within the Association about the importance of ethical issues in the development and use of science and technology." One of the major findings of the project is that more and more technical professional societies are including in their codes of ethics a directive to make safeguarding the public a matter of paramount importance.

Finally, in 1988, AAAS started a new project, *Professional Ethics Report: Newsletter of the* AAAS Committee on Scientific Freedom & Responsibility Professional Society Ethics Group. The same year, AAAS published another report, *Science, Engineering and Ethics: State-of-the-Art* and Future Directions, that reflects not only the concerns of AAAS, but also those of the National Science Foundation—and especially its Ethics and Values Studies (EVS) program.

These efforts are paralleled by similar institutional responses elsewhere. I am aware of some in Canada and West Germany, and I suspect that, almost certainly, others are found in any country that has a large-scale commitment to the promotion of science and technology but which also feels the pressure of an alert citizenry ready to call the technical community to task when irresponsible behaviour occurs in connection with scientific research or engineering development.

Ethicists' Discussions of Scientific Responsibility Issues

These claims about scientific and engineering social responsibility have come from scientific and technical organizations, but they have also been picked up by academic philosophers specializing in applied ethics. The most accessible biblio-graphical listing (which includes books by scientists, engineers, and others, in addition to philosophers) is Carl Mitcham's, "Ethics of Science, Technology, and Medicine."[2] For a slightly older but more comprehensive bibliography, including the whole range of value aspects of technology, see Stephen Cutcliffe, Judith Mistichelli, and Christine Roysdon, *Technology and Values in American Civiliza-tion*.[3]

Mitcham organizes his list under six headings: ethics in science, nuclear ethics (both nuclear weapons and nuclear power), environmental ethics, ethics in medi-cine and bioethics, ethics in information science and computer technologies, and

---

[1]
These proceedings were edited by Rosemary Chaek, Mark Frankel, and Sallie Chafer.

[2]
Carl Mitcham, "Ethics of Science, Technology, and Medicine," in P. Durbin (ed.) *The Best in Literature of Science, Technology, and Medicine*, Vol. 5 of *The Reader's Adviser*, 13th ed., (New York: Bowker, 1988), pp.617–637.

[3]
Stephen Cutcliffe, Judith Mistichelli, and Christine Roysdon, *Technology and Values in American Civilization: A Guide to Information Resources*, (Detroit, Mich.: Gale, 1980).

engineering ethics and ethics of technology. This does not cover all the major technosocial problems I listed at the beginning, but it does suggest that most of them have been discussed in the literature. Among the literature Mitcham surveys the one to which he had to give the most selective treatment is biomedical ethics. That field far outstrips all the others not only in numbers of publications but also in philosophical quality; by now there is a full-scale *Encyclopedia of Bioethics* (4 volumes [1978], currently being updated) and a regularly-updated bibliography (edited by LeRoy Walters), and at least three book length theories of biomedical ethics have been published. The literature in engineering ethics pales by contrast, and no one has yet come close to producing a general theory of that field.

The best philosophical treatment of the ethical responsibilities of scientists and engineers (along with a whole range of other professionals, including physicians and nurses) that I know of is Michael Bayles's *Professional Ethics* (1981, 1989). His primary focus is on professional misconduct and how poor a job professional organizations have done in dealing with it (or even understanding its dimensions).

In an interesting conclusion, Bayles talks about alternatives to the ways professional organizations have gone about assuring compliance with ethics codes. He lists several alternatives: involving more laymen on regulatory boards; more effective enforcement (including changing the grounds for disciplinary action, better reporting of violations, better investigational procedures, and due-process approaches where applicable), and preventive measures—including ethics education during professional training, and collegial pressure or an "ethical climate" in organizations. In a second edition (1989), he adds two more obvious but unspoken alternatives: government regulation and lawsuits.

Another book, an anthology on professional ethics edited by Joan Callahan (*Ethical Issues in Professional Life* [1988]), provides a handy summary of the ethical-theory presuppositions of this approach. With references to Richard Brandt, Norman Daniels, Ronald Dworkin, Kai Nielsen, John Rawls, and Stephen Stich (among others), Callahan proposes as the basic theoretical approach a method of "reflective equilibrium": first propose a set of moral principles, then compare them with basic moral intuitions about appropriate behaviour in concrete situations; sometimes our intuitions will have to be brought in line with moral principles, but at other times moral principles will need to be adjusted to accommodate real life applications of generally accepted moral intuitions.

Callahan's ethical-theory sources include a number of "deontologists" (philosophers for whom moral rules always trump consequences) and utilitarians (for whom consequences determine acceptable rules), but she also refers to an older but recently revived tradition, the "virtue ethics" of Alasdair MacIntyre (see Michael Slote, *Goods and Virtues* [1983]). It is safe (though perhaps controversial) to summarize this approach—which is not idiosyncratic with Callahan but the norm in almost all recent applied ethics work—by saying that Callahan believes that moral reasoning is a matter of subsuming particular cases under general moral rules. The "reflective equilibrium" part is brought in to assure the flexibility of the approach, in contrast to older dogmatic or absolutist philosophical approaches to ethics.

A Social Activist Alternative

In my opinion, these approaches are okay as far as they go—and I find the "virtue ethic" approach especially promising. (For a book that includes it in an especially effective way, see Christopher Stone, *Earth and Other Ethics* [1987].) But it seems to me that there is a still better approach that shows even more promise as an effective way of dealing, in an ethical way, with the major technosocial problems I listed at the beginning. This is the approach once made famous by John Dewey and best articulated by George Herbert Mead (but now largely ignored, even by philosophers like Richard Rorty who claim to have an affinity with Dewey). This approach would have philosophers get involved, working with others—here, especially activist scientists and engineers, along with other activists concerned about problems associated with science and technology—to solve urgent social problems that impede social progress. What Dewey and his fellow American Pragmatists called this approach is "creative intelligence." Its thrust is not, like the philosophers mentioned so far, to make moral decisions from the heights of ethical theory (even in an "applied ethics" or "reflective equilibrium" fashion) but to work out or through the problems, collaboratively, in the most intelligent fashion possible at that particular stage in history, given the body of reliable knowledge available at the time. (Dewey and Mead often spoke of applying "the scientific method to the solution of social problems," and this has led to much misinterpretation—as though they were favoring technocratic social engineering. They did favour social engineering of one sort—progressive liberal social reform—but definitely not of the technocratic sort. For nuanced interpretations of Dewey and Mead, see Ralph W. Sleeper, *The Necessity of Pragmatism* [1986]; Gary Bullert, *The Politics of John Dewey* [1983]; and Hans Joas, *G. H. Mead: A Contemporary Re-Examination of His Thought* [1981, 1985]; Dewey's own formulations are most accessible in *Liberalism and Social Action* [1935]).

While activist pragmatism of this sort is rare today among philosophers in academia, and although the political mood in much of the developed world today seems anti-liberal, progressive liberalism of this sort is by no means dead. It is alive especially in public interest activist groups of all sorts who have taken it upon themselves to do something concrete and practical about the nuclear arms race, about environmental degradation, about problems of poverty and hunger and homelessness (often in the midst of technology-driven abundance), about economic injustices and political corruption (often involving high-technology industries providing weapons or materiel for governments), and so on and on. (For an astute summary of these progressive groups, and their frustrations, see Michael McCann, *Taking Reform Seriously* [1986].)

Mead has an interesting commentary on this sort of approach. Attacking utilitarian ethics as poorly grounded (typically, it assumes a selfish individualism that is at odds with the altruism presupposed by progressive social action) and Kantian ethics as providing no guidance (in the end, real guidance comes from the democratic process of balancing competing values, not from some set of transcendentally deduced Rational Duties)—Mead says *real* ethics is to be found in the progressive social problem solving of the community:

The order of the universe that we live in *is* the moral order.

It has become the moral order by becoming the self-conscious method of the members of a human society... The world that comes to us from the past possesses and controls us. We possess and control the world that we discover and invent.[1]

And the highest order of this ethics-as-progressive-community-problem-solving is to be found in the arena of international cooperation (see chapter 36 of his *Mind, Self, and Society* [1934]). Mead died in 1931 and so could only support international cooperation of the League of Nations sort; but had he lived into another era, he would clearly have supported the United Nations—as Dewey did—and would have, even more so, supported still more effective international bodies that might have a real chance of solving such technosocial problems as the nuclear arms race, transnational pollution, or improper technological impositions on Third World countries by multinational corporations.

I need to end with a reference to the applied ethics literature mentioned earlier. Do such philosophers have nothing to contribute to the solution of technosocial problems? Though Dewey often attacked academic philosophy, I think he and Mead would agree that even the most ivory-tower philosophers *could* make a contribution: clear definitions of the sort that analytical philosophers are so good at providing are often important in solving social problems; so are the other things philosophers of other schools strive for—empirical justification, comprehensiveness, encyclopedic compendia of existing knowledge, even the "authenticity" prized by Existentialist philosophers. *But*—and this is an all-important proviso—these contributions can only be effective if they are somehow communicated to real-life decision-makers. And the best way to do that would be to join in teamwork with others trying to solve urgent problems.

In conclusion, the ethical issues facing us in our technological world are enormous—and the social problems requiring ethical input for their solutions are even more enormous. I believe the most effective way to meet the social and institutional responsibilities of the scientific, technological and biomedical communities is by public interest activism on the part of progressive scientists, engineers, physicians, biomedical researchers, and other technical personnel. They would work either with one another or in activist groups alongside those outside the technical community who are working to solve social problems associated with science, technology, and biomedicine. In the meantime, a good beginning has been made in recent work in applied ethics, but a great deal more could—and should—be done.

DR. PAUL T. DURBIN is Professor of Philosophy at the University of Delaware, USA.

[1] "Scientific Method and the Moral Sciences," *International Journal of Ethics* 33 [1923], p. 247; reprinted in George Herbert Mead, *Selected Writings*, (ed.) A. Reck, (Indianapolis, Ind.: Bobbs-Merrill, 1964), pp.248–266.

References

Ackland, Len, and Steven McGuire, eds. *Assessing the Nuclear Age* (Chicago: University of Chicago Press, 1986).

Bayles, Michael D. *Professional Ethics* (2d ed.; Belmont, Calif.: Wadsworth, 1989; original, 1981).

Bullert, Gary. *The Politics of John Dewey* (Buffalo, N.Y.: Prometheus, 1983).

Callahan, Joan C., ed. *Ethical Issues in Professional Life* (New York: Oxford University Press, 1988).

Chalk, Rosemary, Mark S. Frankel, and Sallie B. Chafer. *AAAS Professional Ethics Project: Professional Ethics Activities in the Scientific and Engineering Societies* (Washington, D.C.: American Association for the Advancement of Science, 1980).

Committee on Scientific Freedom and Responsibility. *Scientific Freedom and Responsibility* (Washington, D.C.: American Association for the Advancement of Science, 1975).

Cutcliffe, Stephen, Judith A. Mistichelli, and Christine M. Roysdon, *Technology and Values in American Civilization: A Guide to Information Resources* (Detroit, Mich.: Gale, 1980).

Dewey, John. *Liberalism and Social Action* (New York: Putnam's, 1935).

Frankel, Mark S., ed. *Science, Engineering and Ethics: State-of-the-Art and Future Directions* (Washington, D.C.: American Association for the Advancement of Science, 1988).

Grodzins, Morton, and Eugene Rabinowitch, eds. *The Atomic Age: Scientists in National and World Affairs; Articles from the Bulletin of the Atomic Scientists, 1945–1962* (New York: Basic Books, 1963).

Joas, Hans. *G. H. Mead: A Contemporary Re-Examination of His Thought* (Cambridge, Mass.: MIT Press, 1985; German original, 1980).

McCann, Michael W. *Taking Reform Seriously: Perspectives on Public Interest Liberalism* (Ithaca, N.Y.: Cornell University Press, 1986).

Mead, George Herbert. *Mind, Self, and Society: From the Standpoint of a Social Behaviorist* (Chicago: University of Chicago Press, 1934).

"Scientific Method and the Moral Sciences," *International Journal of Ethics* 33 (1923): 229–247; reprinted in George Herbert Mead, *Selected Writings*, ed. A. Reck (Indianapolis, Ind.: Bobbs-Merrill, 1964), pp. 248–266.

Mitcham, Carl. "Ethics of Science, Technology, and Medicine," in P. Durbin, ed., *The Best in the Literature of Science, Technology, and Medicine*, volume 5 of *The Reader's Adviser*, 13th ed. (New York: Bowker, 1988), pp. 617–637.

Reich, Warren T., ed. *The Encyclopedia of Bioethics*, 4 volumes (New York: Macmillan and Free Press, 1978).

Sleeper, Ralph W. *The Necessity of Pragmatism: John Dewey's Conception of Philosophy* (New Haven, Conn.: Yale University Press, 1986).

Slote, Michael. *Goods and Virtues* (New York: Oxford University Press, 1983).

Stone, Christopher D. *Earth and Other Ethics: The Case for Moral Pluralism* (New York: Harper & Row, 1987).

UNIT II
GLOBAL SURVIVAL

CHAPTER 5 VIGNETTE (OPPOSITE PAGE):

Detail from "The Unicorn in Captivity," seventh panel of The Unicorn Tapestries: 15th Century, Franco-Flemish.

The tapestries are allegories of how 15C. Europeans interpreted relationships among humans, plants, animals, and their landscapes. This tapestry depicts the yearly cycle and the sexual powers of plants and animals. The unicorn represents a synthesis of icons, be they the spirit of wilderness, symbols of fertility and abundance, death and resurrection, or the advent of spring to winter. The tree to which the unicorn is tethered is the pomegranate, identified biblically with the Tree of Life.

5   *Vernon G. Thomas*

Science, Technology, and Environment

Technology, coarsely defined as intentional human manipulation of components of the environment, is integral in all cultures. It is therefore axiomatic that *Homo sapiens* has had an unusual impact on its environment attributable to the cultured nature of this species. In this essay the principal reasons why a sour relationship has developed between technology and environment will be outlined. Providing solutions to problems first requires a correct diagnosis of the root causes of the problem. It is the misapplication of some technology, or inadvisable criteria concerning its application, which has impaired human-environment relationships, and not the technology itself. There is an extraordinary need for technology which minimizes the impacts of human existence upon environments and which promotes the vigour of renewable resource systems. Old technologies are not always passé, nor future technology pregnant with promise. Sound environmental technology will heed the properties of ecosystems and be introduced when Society has defined and reconciled itself to a truly sustainable relationship with its environment.

Historically one can trace over millennia, in every continent, the widespread use of fire by tribes not only to catch game but also to maintain habitats in their early stages of productivity. Thus certain features of the global environment are artefacts of human culture, such as the large feudal hardwood forests and hedgerow systems of Europe, fire-regulated grasslands, heaths and commons. Today we accept these quasi-natural systems because they have their own unique assemblage of species and because they have persisted across centuries. However, they are very different from the native systems they usurp, and, without continued human practices, they would revert to a different state.

From the Bronze Age to the present, one can see the residual impacts of metal smelting in many parts of the world. Large-scale deforestation throughout the Mediterranean lands and Europe attended the Bronze and Iron Ages. The toxins released by smelting sulphide ores and tailings from lead mines exerted the same effects two millennia ago as they do now.

What has changed during the intervening period is the extent and rate of increase of such activities as the human population increases and science spawns new technologies at unprecedented rates. Human relationships with the environment have remained, ultimately, unchanged, despite rapid cultural evolution. The fundamental links are represented by nutrition and respiration, but also, importantly, through aesthetics and spirituality. All technologies have been predicated on human imagination, and although some have, unwittingly, compromised the integrity of the relationship with the environment, human imagination is the sole means for repairing that relationship. Although the human species has experienced waves of civilization, humans still comprise a biological core covered incompletely by a veneer of civilized culture, with the result that many human actions belie our intellectual capacity. Thus many of the technologies that have been developed complement mainly the biological aspects of human nature, be they aggression, competition, resource acquisition, creature comfort or longevity. If technology is going to be used constructively in our interactions with environment, then it must be preceded by a reconciliation of the biological and intellectual sides of human nature.

The negative environmental impacts that technology has produced can be traced to several fundamental precepts. Pioneers in the New World and Antipodes during the 18th and 19th centuries generally acknowledged an adversarial relationship with their environment. The passage in Genesis of the Old Testament wherein God gave Man dominion over the Earth and its Creatures has rarely been interpreted as custodianship with preservation and conservation, but domination, harnessing and sanctioned exploitation. This has led to the conceptual divorce of humans from nature, and potentiated the fallacy that human existence is not integral with the environment. The same attitude is the raison d'être for regarding natural wealth as the sole basis for social economic gain.

The last century, in particular, has witnessed an interaction among the concept of progress, social change, technology, economics, and Judeo-Christian religion. Science, as a discipline serving the understanding of natural phenomena, has shifted, significantly, to support the technologies and ambitions of nations. In so doing it has become a remarkably successful employer, lobbyist, and vested interest group, but has often lost its ethic and internal moderation.

Extreme specialization and reductionist approaches have led to the uncoupling of scientific disciplines, sub-disciplines and topics within them. This extreme specialization in science and technology is attended by an equally restricted sense of obligation and responsibility to the parent discipline on the part of its practitioners, whether it be in medicine, agriculture or environmental sciences. Synthesis is not given the same priority as analysis. There is a *gestalt* in biology which is the essence of its understanding, whether one is dealing with human biology or the functioning of environments. This necessitates that analysis be conducted with a view to synthesis and that specific technological advances be assessed, ultimately, from a holistic perspective, especially in agriculture and environmental biology. The biological sciences must begin to re-couple their approach to research and technology development, and acquire the candour to assess mandates and directions. This should not be the sole responsibility of others, but the ethical responsibility of biologists. It is often said that the great breadth and depth of the biological-environmental sciences precludes synthetic competence. However, there are physicists whose minds transcend the many components of Big Bang Theories and other celestial events. It takes no great mind to see the relations between tropical soil erosion and depressed food security, or connections among Brazilian land tenure, forest destruction, and its impacts upon the El Niño Southern Oscillation and climate changes. Rather there has been no selection for such capabilities among biological scientists.

The 17th century taxonomist Carl von Linné (and later, others such as Darwin) recognized that natural environments had their unique economies, however this collective realization has not permeated modern economic theory of natural resource management. This is important in that economic criteria are presently paramount in the development of technologies which affect environments. Dahlberg[1] indicated that renewable biotic resources are far more important for sustaining human cultures than non-renewable, finite resources. Yet the economic philosophy and technology used to deal with both are basically extractive in the short-term. Much technological development in the area of natural resources has concentrated on the efficiency of harvest, extraction or catch. Forests are viewed as "lumber in waiting," and the diverse productive contributions of living trees to environments are little recognized and rarely modelled economically or included in modern technological practices.

The report of The World Commission on Environment and Development[2] states clearly that sustainable relationships with environments must recognize a reciprocity, or equilibrium, between the economy of natural, biotic resources and the economy of Society. The environment has to be invested in if it is expected to produce into the future. Nature has supported Society well in the past and has the potential to do so in the future, provided its capital is not eroded, whether it be forests, ocean fisheries or fertile soil. Nature is unaware of the fiscal quarter or the financial year, and produces, acquires capital, and yields dividends over a wide array of time courses. It is thus essential that the technology of fisheries agriculture and forestry be not assessed solely on the efficacy of converting natural wealth to economic gain, but also on their ability to enhance natural resource capital and productivity.

The costs of detrimental consequences of intensive forestry agricultural and fisheries technology are presently externalized for all of society to absorb, so inflating the apparent efficiency of certain technologies. These externalities should be internalized so that the real efficiency and value of practices can be assessed by society.

Western governments have spent inordinate sums of money to raise the apparent productivity of farm systems using intensive, energy and chemically-dependent practices. In intensive practices components of natural environments are viewed as competitors and natural contributions to production have been eclipsed. Now modern technology-based inputs replace biological inputs into production, and the contributions of nature have been made redundant. The resulting high production rates of crops and animals have not been obtained cheaply, despite the low prices of food. Collectively, the profligate use of energy, adverse impacts upon soil, high farmer bankruptcy rates, changes in rural society and absenteeism of land tenure render this approach to food production unsustainable, whether judged on economic or ecological criteria. Only the subsidies from other productive solvent sectors of national economies enable the intensive practices to continue.

There are alternate technologies in agriculture which have produced consistently over generations. The crop rotation techniques introduced during the British

---

[1] K.A. Dahlberg, 1987. *Conservation Biology 1* (4): 311–322.

[2] Gro H. Brundtland, (Chairperson), *Our Common Future*, (New York: Oxford University Press, 1987, World Commission on Environment and Development).

Agricultural Revolution are still as valid and vital today as at their inception. There is no simple, substitute for integrated, mixed animal-crop-pasture schemes of farming. Agriculture that is sympathetic to the environment displays practices which deliberately involve non-agricultural lands as adjuncts in diversified production. These are water bodies which assist the maintenance of water-tables and water flux through soil during dry periods. Hedges and tree windbreaks mediate water cycling, and provide habitat for species which may be involved in crop pollination, biological control of crop pests, and refugia for soil organisms. Rather than view such features as components of an archaic scheme of production, research should be done on these natural structures so that their potential contribution to production can be raised.

The continuous monocropping of a narrow range of field crops, protected by synthetic biocides and nurtured by heavy fertilization, is an artefact of a post World War II technology whose success is likely short-lived. The Green Revolution using the same technologies has enjoyed short-term success, but already shows signs of failure because it has been superimposed upon an environment, not integrated with it. Promises of technological developments which offer yet more returns to society need careful scrutiny. The Laws of Thermodynamics apply fully to human environmental practices because they involve ecological principles[1]. Yet, as Georgescu-Roegen[2] has indicated, modern economic paradigms and the technologies they support, appear reluctant to accept that there are real limits on the recovery of inputs in productive systems. Perhaps the most effective way to maximize returns from productive environments over time, is to promote diversity of production, whether in aquatic, forest, or agricultural systems. This philosophy is centuries old: Western nations have temporarily (and perhaps conveniently) overlooked it.

Although earlier paragraphs appear critical of some technological applications, it is axiomatic that new technology and practices will mediate future human environmental relations. To be sustainable they must be rationalized to serve the long-term interests of both humans and environments. Space research has advanced knowledge of the planets and also provided satellite systems which are invaluable for detailed analysis of Earth's lands and climates. Although exploration is exciting, we need the development of technologies which enable life to exist more assuredly on Earth rather than escape from it. New technologies which minimize human impacts on environments are long overdue. Often this does not derive from a dearth of scientific knowledge, but more from social lassitude and competing economies. Recycling technology is still in its infancy, yet can alleviate severe environmental burdens. No North American city can boast sophisticated sewage treatment systems, yet they provide a huge opportunity for new microbial biotechnology, engineering design, and nutrient capture techniques. Social priorities now ensure their uncompetitiveness with the technology used for building domed stadia for professional athletes. The great likelihood of global change

1

   D.E. Koshland, Jr., 1987. *Science.* 237 (4810): 9.

2

   N. Georgescu-Roegen, *The Entropy Law and the Economic Process*, (Cambridge, Massachusetts: Harvard University Press, 1971).

attributable, partly, to excessive burning of fossil fuels, should catalyze techno-logical developments in alternate energy forms, whether safer nuclear power, or geothermal power. However this catalyst still responds to the OPEC pricing policy for oil.

Tremendous potential for plant technology exists in the area of food production, especially to produce varieties which flourish in rotational schemes and mixed species associations. If we recognize soil as an ecosystem, then selection for plant varieties and growing techniques which enhance its intrinsic productivity is as important as selection for just the harvestable fraction. Prodigious opportunities exist for developing yet more chemical attractants for certain insect pests, espe-cially where there are no imminent biological controls. They are highly localized, species-specific, and devoid of the serious detractions facing most pesticide operations. Moreover, these attractants provide an alternate product for the chem-ical industry.

Rapid population growth poses persistent challenges to environmental vitality. Some politicians and economists may see this as the stimulus which evokes a scientific-technological solution to the initial problem (i.e. Malthus was totally wrong). However, naive faith in the ability of applied science to provide solutions continuously serves no one's interests, especially given the historical record. There are limits to growth in some continents which are already blatant. The concept of life in a no-growth society, although temporarily discarded, will soon have to be revived in the interests of sustainability. The idea that western styles of intensive food production applied worldwide can support over 15 billion people, has not assessed the adverse impact that it will have upon the environment, nor that of the extra humans. It presupposes that food, alone, suffices, and assumes that climate, air, and water remain conducive to life. The quantity and quality of human life are not always commensurate, irrespective of technology. Aesthetics cannot be over-looked, in that the vitality of natural environments relates positively to the well being of all human society.[1]

The oil spill near Valdez, Alaska, in early 1989, strikes a very discordant note. Despite the abundant oil recovery technology and the means to deploy it, nothing was done when such technology could have been effective. Environmental inter-ests lost to a lack of will, or worse, to the competitive economic costs of keeping such technology in readiness. Environmental integrity has to be perceived to be worth the investment. There is an abundance of science to support that assertion: the imagination to think in a new way is limiting.

DR. V. G. THOMAS is Professor of Zoology at the University of Guelph.

---

[1] D.W. Ehrenfeld, *The Arrogance of Humanism*, (New York: Oxford University Press, 1978).

6   *George Lindsey and Geoffrey Pearson*

Technology, Peace, and Security

Although technology may be changing quickly, the human motivations, interactions and ethics that have determined questions of peace and security for hundreds of years do not change as fast. We should remember that, from Roman times through the Middle Ages to Napoleon, warfare was one of the standard and perfectly acceptable means of conducting international relations. Although some religions (presumably the teachers of ethics) preached against war, most did not, and they all did more to cause wars than to prevent them.

Perhaps for the same reasons that animals restrain their combative behaviour so as to preserve the continued existence of their species, men put limitations to the use of force against one another. With few exceptions, victors who had the physical power to completely destroy their opponents refrained from so doing, contenting themselves with an adjustment of state boundaries or economic retribution. Starvation of an opponent besieged in a fortified town, or dependent on supply over the sea, was an acceptable measure, with the expectation that the victims would surrender, then eat and live on. As territoriality was at the core of conflict, conquest, rather than extermination was usually paramount.

Military technology was simple and easily copied. There was not much difference between a fully-equipped warrior and his opponent, or between offence and defence. The security of a state depended on numbers, and numbers often depended on diplomacy and the forging of suitable alliances. In Napoleonic times, the demand for numbers produced the practice of national conscription for military service. The increased size of armies placed even greater dependence on logistics which became more important than the quality of armaments.

The rapid technological development since the American Civil War but particularly since World War I has produced new ethical problems. Extension of economic blockades through unrestricted submarine warfare created great indignation, though not so much because of the starvation which it was intended to bring as for the reason that civilian passengers who were citizens of non-belligerent countries were being drowned. Poison gas raised general revulsion, but stimulated the aggrieved parties to reciprocate in kind. In the aftermath, treaties were signed to outlaw chemical warfare and it was not used again on any significant scale until many years after World War II. However, resumption of unrestricted submarine warfare in World War II did not generate much ethical objection.

During World War I, defence was so strong that it produced a stalemate situation and a terrible war of attrition—and "position" that was only reversed by the highly mobile technology of *Blitzkrieg*. The latter was developed in the 1930s and demonstrated with great success in 1940. An offensive by properly armed and trained troops could succeed in overrunning and destroying opponents of equal numerical strength. The subsequent development of techniques for paratroop and amphibious operations removed the security of islands and fortified coasts. But, the most important strategic development attributable to technology was the capability to attack and destroy centres of population and industry without first having to defeat a defending army, navy, or air force. This was the technique of blanket aerial bombardment of the enemy's cities and industrial centres. While all the bombers did not get through, enough of them did to inflict terrible damage, and the associated loss of life was mostly civilian, albeit enemy civilians.

Whether for reasons of ethics or hard-headed *realpolitik*, following World War II, the victorious Allies did not attempt to extract reparations from the losers, but proceeded to rehabilitate them into the world economy.

Technological Development and Nuclear Warfare

The two most important technological developments of modern times originated during World War II but came into full fruition in subsequent decades. These were the creation of nuclear weapons (first fission and then fusion bombs) and of accurate long-range rockets able to deliver these over intercontinental distances. Clearly, the destructive capabilities of the conventional strategic bomber of 1944–45 were now multiplied by a factor so enormous that a nation with intercontinental missiles with nuclear warheads could destroy any opponent, anywhere in the world, with no defence being possible. Against this threat, the only logical countermeasure (short of submission) was to ensure that retaliation could be delivered by the same means, on a scale so terrible that the original aggressor would be deterred from the initial strike. Whether strategic deterrence is ethical or not, for some years, it has offered the only possible—and rational—means of providing some security against an opponent armed with long-range nuclear weapons. A very satisfactory aspect of this state of mutual nuclear deterrence that has prevailed during the past quarter-century is that there have been no wars among the states possessing nuclear weapons.

If the mission of ethics is to provide for a civilized existence, if existence depends on survival, and survival in civilized circumstances depends on strategic deterrence, then ethics should owe a certain respect to strategic deterrence. It is a kind of "consequential morality." Removal of the nuclear threat by negotiated disarmament could be ethically satisfying in itself. However, it would be necessary to examine the consequent state of world peace and security as well as the ethical foundation that would prevail in the absence of nuclear deterrence.

Strategic Goals for Future Military Technology

Even in a world where nuclear weapons acquire a low profile, one can set three main strategic goals for future military technology. One is to keep strategic nuclear deterrence stable. Such deterrence should be both against the temptation of launching a nuclear attack in a crisis to gain a strategic advantage, and against the risks of inadvertently launching weapons, whether from miscalculation, misunderstanding, disobedience, false alarm, or accident. As long as nuclear weapons exist, such goals can hardly be considered unethical. Technology has made vital contributions to both of these objectives. The vulnerability of land-based weapons has been decreased by placing them in hardened underground silos, and of sea-based weapons by deploying them in quiet nuclear-powered submarines. The survivability of the command and control systems has been improved by building alternate airborne command posts and redundant communication networks. Fail-safe procedures and equipment have made unauthorized arming of nuclear weapons virtually impossible. However, technological developments can also be destabilizing instead of stabilizing, and can foment expensive but self-neutralizing competition.

Another goal would be to change the technology of conventional war so that the advantage would lie with defence over offence. Inasmuch as aggression is linked to offence, it should be ethical to provide the capability to resist effectively.

A third goal for technology would be to strengthen the ability to verify that security agreements are being honoured by all parties concerned. It cannot be unethical to build confidence that treaties on which security depends are not being subverted. Related to this last function is a general improvement in communication and understanding, likely to reduce suspicion and promote peace. Through satellite-borne photography and the relay of telemetry, technology has provided the means to verify the most important agreements on arms control of strategic weapons, both as regards deployment of operational systems and testing of systems under development.

Shaping the Future

Technology will certainly be applied to the development of advanced conventional military weapons and equipment. Changes are to be expected in the operational capabilities of certain systems in relation to their natural opposing systems. For example, surface-to-air missiles seem to be getting the better of aircraft, including helicopters. This trend could be reversed by stealth technology. Anti-tank guided missiles are progressing faster than improvements to tank armour. Anti-ship missiles have the advantage over surface ships. Submarines are now so quiet that antisubmarine warfare is becoming even more difficult than it was. However, while one could take the utopian line that it is unethical to make any military equipment work better than it does now, there seems to be little to distinguish one particular application from another on ethical grounds.

Apart from its potential for the prevention of war, or for peace-keeping, technology will, of course, influence the character of such wars which are not prevented. Most of these are likely to be fought with conventional weapons, and by armies from developing nations. The belligerents may have industrialized countries as patrons, or as suppliers on a commercial basis. The most advanced types of tanks, aircraft, and warships are unlikely to be involved so that the relevant technology will be more concerned with simplicity, ruggedness, maintainability, reliability, and cheapness than with maximum performance.

Depending on the terrain, transportation could be very important. However, the Vietnam war showed that while one side can get great help from airlift, air support, helicopters, night vision devices, defoliants, cluster bombs, and many other products of modern technology, it may not be enough to win the war. While some ethical objections were raised regarding the methods employed by the United

States in Vietnam (e.g. Agent Orange), these were overshadowed by disagreement with the strategic purposes behind the war itself.

The organization, training, methods, and weapons designed for continuous warfare between large uniformed military units are not well suited to lower intensity operations such as counterinsurgency or guerrilla warfare, or peace-keeping. In these latter situations, it may be more important to pacify or convert the opponents, or to obtain the cooperation of the indigenous population, than to destroy identified enemy formations. Collection of intelligence and choice of an appropriate psychological campaign is likely to be more important than the selection of weapons and equipment. The problems of dealing with political dissent, ideology, and pacification are likely to be related more to ethics than to technology.

The most advanced technologies and the weapons systems they produce will remain under the control of the most highly industrialized countries. For example, the tendency is for the number of firms able to produce high-performance military aircraft to decrease, even in the most highly developed nations. The countries manufacturing the most advanced weapons face the choice of restricting sales and maintaining their superiority, or making money and selling abroad, thus allowing weapons to fall into the hands of future enemies. In some cases, there are "restricted lists" of countries whose social or political behaviour is considered undesirable, and to which sales of all or certain kinds of military equipment are forbidden. The five states who own nuclear weapons are firm in their desire to prevent future proliferation. But these policies have been adopted for reasons of security rather than ethics.

We may soon be reaching the point where modern weapons make war between opponents, both of whom are equipped with the most advanced versions, either impossible or unwinnable. If the governments of the great powers come to this conclusion, negotiations to reduce or eliminate weapons of mass destruction may actually succeed. However, if agreements are to be reached, the technology to verify them will need to be adequate. Although they did not conclude such an agreement at their meeting in Reykjavik in 1986, Ronald Reagan and Mikhail Gorbatchev indicated that they entertained long-term goals of this nature. More-over, as other threats to human well-being and security mount (especially threats to the ecology of the earth), both the costs and the irrelevance of sophisticated weapons become more obvious.

On the other hand, growing disparities in the way people live, leading in turn to "demographic tidal waves," are likely to stimulate a greater resort to violence. Technology has made low-level violence and terrorism much easier to initiate and sustain. If technology has made the abolition of war at least thinkable, and certainly desirable, then at the highest level of destructiveness, it may also have vastly increased the obstacles to reaching that "positive peace" to which the great religions have long aspired.

DR. G. LINDSEY is former Chief, Defence Research Establishment of the Canadian National Defence Department.

G. PEARSON is former Ambassador to the Soviet Union and former Director of the Canadian Institute for International Peace and Security.

Further Reading

The Harvard Nuclear Study Group. *Living with Nuclear Weapons* (Toronto: Bantam, 1983).

Paret, Peter, (ed.). *Makers of Modern Strategy. From Machiavelli to the Nuclear Age* (New Jersey: Princeton, 1986).

Woolsey, R. James, (ed.). *Nuclear Arms: Ethics, Strategy, Politics* (San Francisco: ICS Press, 1984).

Nye, Joseph. *Nuclear Ethics* (New York: Free Press, 1986).

Kirk, Elizabeth. *Technology, Security, and Arms Control for the 1990s* (Washington: American Association for the Advancement of Science, 1988).

Nora Cebotarev

7

Technology and Development

Most ethical deliberations on technology and development revolve mainly around issues of technology diffusion or transfer. Generally speaking, technology creation is considered as an unquestionable "good," a symptom of progress. Underlying values and ethical issues of technology creation are seldom addressed. It is proposed in this article that the most basic ethical questions in the technology-development relation need to be addressed in the process of technology creation. If technology is seen as a social product embodying the socio-economic and political interests and worldviews of its creators, it is insufficient to monitor the side-effects of technology diffusion in the developing world. The examination of value assumptions underlying technology production is basic. We need to acknowledge that we are diffusing our own socio-cultural system with the technology we export.

It is at the inception of its creation that the discussion of ethics regarding technology and development need to begin. It is also the point where social controls over technology production can be restored.

This brief article first reviews the technology-development relationship. Later it presents a sample of humanistic approaches to development ethics and concludes with an alternative ethical and feminist approach to the ambiguous technology-development relationship.

Development and Technology

Development is a term with a variety of meanings. However it always contains the idea that certain activities could lead to socio-economic "betterment," to "progress" and to the improvement of people's "quality of life." This is the normative aspect of development thought and action.

Ethical problems arise when "experts" unilaterally decide on development goals, and on what the "quality of life" of others should be. This often results in the disruption of people's lives and disturbs their socio-economic and natural environments.

When referring to "developing countries," the actually existing "development" goals are seldom in tune with the realities of their socio-economic environment. Development planners often view development in "lofty" terms which implies reaching or replicating the socio-economic conditions existing in the industrial world. In the meantime, many developing countries have not yet reached the stage of attaining a state of sustainable survival for the majority of their population. Moreover, development rarely takes place on a national scale. More often than not a small elite minority reaps the benefits while the vast majority see their living conditions deteriorate. Sustainable development can therefore not be measured uniformly. It is specific to class, gender and the culture of the socio-economic environment. Whether explicitly or implicitly, the modern, industrial world still remains the ideal to be attained by development efforts and it continues to be the yardstick against which development outcomes are assessed. The degree of satisfaction of "needs" and "wants," as expressed by individual possession of material (food, shelter, TVs, cars, etc.) and social (education, health, access to services, political participation, etc.) goods—which in the West has reached historically unprecedented high levels—become the indicators of modern conditions.

Technology is often credited with being the single most outstanding factor which has facilitated the emergence of the modern, Western industrial world. (The role of Western economic and political links with the less developed countries are less often considered.) Technology is also credited with creating the high standards of living in Western societies. In fact, as technological determinists—who see technology as a progressive force—would have it, today's technology has acquired a dynamics of its own which cannot be stopped but must be obeyed and followed, lest we get in the way of progress. From this perspective, technology is seen as the best if not the only solution to most development problems. It is not surprising then, that among various "development" actions, the diffusion or the transfer of modern technology holds such a prominent and privileged place.

It is true historically that technology, as socio-cultural process or product, has played important roles in the improvement of human life. In the past, however, the production of technological know-how was a collective enterprise, based on "substantive rationality," on the distillation of a group's own life experience in meeting survival needs. Technology then was subordinated to the group's cultural values and needs. The use and application of technology was socially controlled, that is, technology was only used in response to social needs. For example, hybrid corn was discovered many centuries before its widespread cultivation arose in response to population pressures in central Mexico (MacNeish 1961, 1964; Flaherty 1972; Mangelsdorf et al., 1964).

The production of modern technology, however, responds to a different logic. Formal, instrumental rationality is substituted for substantive concerns; efficiency has priority over social consequences. Commercial viability and profit override considerations of social impact. Today, the historical relationship between social needs and technological response is often inverted; social needs are created by mass media, advertisements and education, in response to newly invented technological products, gadgets, processes and know-how. Existing social controls are ineffective and retroactive. New, preventive, pro-active controls over the values underlying technology production are advocated by some (Baram, 1971: 353).

The content/function of technology is never value-neutral nor culture-free, it reflects the interests, priorities and worldviews of its creators. Technology embodies these values and tends to reproduce them, even if imperfectly, in the developing world. This makes modern technology's social impact very significant and more "appropriate" in some societies than in others. In some socio-cultural settings our technology can become truly dysfunctional, if not outright damaging. Its ecological impact may be even more devastating than in our own society.

For example, North American labour saving, agricultural mechanization reflects the high cost and scarcity of labour existing in this continent. In North America, mechanization became a crucial factor in our extraordinary agricultural productivity. And it has facilitated the transition from an agrarian to an industrial society. For countries with abundant labour supplies and limited employment opportunities, this technology is certainly not the most appropriate. It erodes the soil and displaces farm labour. And since modern industry tends to be highly automated, mechanization only enlarges the number of the unemployed who lack the means for purchasing the outputs produced by this very technology. This has occurred in several Latin American countries (de Janvry et al., 1988: Jordan et al. 1989). Another example of the diffusion of our technology and set of values can be seen in the demise of the Brazilian rainforest.

While some technological inventions may truly benefit the majorities in a country, others only serve the economic interests of a few and increase the disparity between the rich and the poor. Development research has documented innumerable cases of such technological misfit. Moreover, modern technology used in Third World countries, requires, more often than not, foreign inputs and modern expert know-how for efficient use and management. It needs parts for maintenance and good repair of tools and equipment. And modern organizational infrastructure and congruent for rational application. This effectively creates technological dependence of non-industrial countries on the modern world and militates against national self-government and self-determination.

Thus, the diffusion of modern technology, although at times conducive to increases of productivity, health and standards of living, also tends to endanger the ecology and disrupts the cultural fabric of developing societies. In many cases, the acritical application of our technology negates the very process which it attempts to promote by limiting a nation's control over her own destiny and future.

A Sampling of Humanist Ethics

The recognition of the ambiguous relationship between technology and development has created ethical concerns which have yet to be fully resolved.

The conventional, pragmatic way of approaching the technology-development question is generally framed in terms of various brands of moral relativism, of which "dialogic" or plain "muddling through" are the favorites (Crocker, 1980: 19–23). In the first approach, modern (expert) values and traditional, (indigenous) values are discussed on an ongoing basis, so that compromises and agreements can be reached regarding the development process. In the second, contextually delimited possibilities are acted upon in order to attain an incremental approximation to the desired goals.

Less conventional approaches to ethical issues of development practice are proposed by humanists in the social sciences. Humanists are dissatisfied with the cavalier treatment given to the social/human side-effects of development by technological determinists or by those who believe that economic growth, like human health, is a self-justifying end. Humanist approaches start from a moral stance centering on human decision and action in the development process. They recognize the political nature of development decisions, even when cast in technological terms. They also recognize the ethical issues raised for developing societies by developments of the modern world.

Peter L. Berger (1974), a conservative humanist, says "No political ethics worthy of that name can avoid the issues of Third World development." In a fairly conventional way, Berger separates science from political ethics and defends a value-free scientific stance. He argues for the debunking of both the myths of capitalism and socialism. However as a humanist, he is sensitive to the social disruptions produced by development and with the way all human beings interpret and assign meaning to their experiences, to what they define as a desirable "quality of life." Berger suggests two principles for an ethics of development: it ought to be assessed by a "calculus of pain" and a "calculus of meaning." The "calculus of pain" directs us to look at the human costs of development. Is the cost of gains in social and economic well-being justified or excessive? The "calculus of meaning" suggests that development goals must be meaningful for the target population. If these goals are culturally disruptive and meaningless to people, such development is not worth promoting.

Berger suggests that development be based on "hard-nosed" objective research and "hard-nosed" utopian imagination. While not addressing technological issues directly, Berger provides useful criteria for ethical assessment of development work. However, he fails to outline a practical strategy for implementing his program. How will the utopian imagination be married to hard-nosed, value-free analysis? Who will define what a "meaningful society" is and how will it inform development policies? Is he not advocating "more of the same," more of what we have been doing for the last three decades with less than clear-cut positive outcomes?

Denis Goulet, a liberal humanist, argues that "development is not a self-validating end"; if seen as such, it can result in "anti-development." He thinks that reciprocity between the developed and the developing world is essential. The following principles are guides he sets out for development work:

- The proposed (development) changes must be congenial with the perceived values of the population.
- The judgement of the population must be respected as to how controls are exercised over the direction, speed and the precise agency of the planned change the population undergoes.
- The population must be urged to evaluate the ethical merits of proposed changes before steps are taken to implement them.

Goulet argues that development often fails (turns into anti-development) because of the prevailing view that the "goodness" of economic growth is unquestionable and self-evident; because development goals are not analyzed in intrinsic terms but only as they contribute to or deter from modernization.

Goulet sees development as a means for enriching the "quality of human life." As a humanist, he argues for a development which respects cultural integrity and provides people with "enough material goods to become more fully human," rather than simply augmenting material possessions or endorsing economic growth. Goulet's strategy for development practitioners is: to distinguish the core from the expendable values in a culture and respect the first; to find out who are the legitimate agents of value formulation; to discover the people's criteria for optimum modality, direction and rate of change, and to build the development strategy on this. He suggests that development practitioners adopt a critical stance vis-à-vis development goals; that they examine the development process from "inside out" (that is from the perspective of those who are being "developed"); that they isolate values and countervalues; that they prepare guidelines for different behavioral sectors which will constitute the normative strategies to be followed in a variety of areas; and that they begin building a coherent theoretical framework in which fragmentary constructs can be unified around a few interrelated analytical concepts.

Goulet proposes a participatory, culture sensitive approach to the issues of development ethics. In his view reciprocity has to be established between the "experts" and those who undergo development; in order to decrease social distance between the two, Goulet counsels experts to acknowledge their vulnerability to the target group. Goulet's approach undermines the power of the "experts," which is left intact, if not strengthened, in Berger's strategy.

For radical humanists like Orlando Fals-Borda, development ethics call for a stronger stand. He argues that the stance of the detached scholar and the development practitioner are contradictory and irreconcilable. Those who wish to espouse both delude themselves. Development workers must take sides. They must choose whether they wish to be part of the problem (if they do not challenge the status quo) or of the solution. Fals-Borda thinks that science and technology, as far as they reflect the dominant, predatory capitalist ideology are part of the problem.

Consequent with his own views, Fals-Borda chooses to ally himself with the oppressed. He argues that development practitioners have to examine situations with a new objectivity derived from the application of the scientific method to the problematic and contradictory expression of reality as experienced by common, oppressed people. He claims that the value-free scientific stance ignores this reality and supports the interests of the experts, the privileged elites and the industrial societies. Fals-Borda wishes to rid the social sciences of this exploitative nature and shape them into a tool of development for the majority. Moreover, Fals-Borda accuses conventional social sciences of a conservative bias because they attempt to avoid contradictions, conflict and confrontations with the status quo and because they err in labelling as subversive all those who act extra-legally, who challenge an existing order, no matter what the conditions of justice are in the society where they are challenged. Fals-Borda believes that there are times when subversion is justified, if not required.

Fals-Borda's work restores subversion to its ethical status. In his search to understand the processes of social transformation, Fals-Borda reviews the history of many significant religious and social changes, such as those induced by Christianity. He finds that without exception, their initiators are first seen as subversive before legitimately recognized as great reformers. Fals-Borda maintains that "subversion is a forerunner of social construction, it is a vital force in the transformation of passivity and exploitation into human dignity and liberation." For him subversion is a legitimate part of historical social change processes to overturn entrenched, unjust conditions. Fals-Borda endorses subversion's objectives of change, praises the valour of its heroes, and reinterprets it as a socially constructive and morally justifiable category. The main values underlying his ethics of development are justice and dignity for the common people. He recommends that researchers espouse the cause of the oppressed, that they conduct research with common people, on subjects which can bring them benefits and justice. For him development work must contribute to genuine social transformation and not to greater inequality, dependence and ecological damage. Although Fals-Borda does not address the ethics of technology/development directly, his ethics can easily incorporate such questions.

In some ways, Fals-Borda's stance is an ethics of defense, that is a defense of the common people against cultural invasion, against exploitation, inequality and foreign domination, an ethics which could lead to indigenous development. Above all his ethics attempts to balance out or to reverse the power relations between "experts" and people, between the developed and the developing worlds. However, this approach is just as gender-blind as the approaches reviewed earlier, reflecting this basic deficiency of the social and ethical theories on which they are built.

Alternative Ethics for Development

From the above discussion of approaches to technology/development ethics, it can be gathered that little thought is given to the underlying values imbedded in modern technology and to the societal values that this technology tacitly transmits to the developing world.

Modernity is the value complex on which our technology is built; its societal meaning has been characterized as the "loss of community" and the creation of the "homeless mind" (Bell, 1972; Berger, 1972). Modernity represents an extremely individualistic social order, an agglomeration of detached self-seeking individuals competing with each other in efforts to maximize their self-interest, disregarding social ties and affective bonds, lest they be considered irrational. The spread of this worldview has led to modernization and to considerable accumulation of wealth among the upper strata of many developing societies. At the same time it has led to a deterioration of the quality of life in terms of safety, security, mutual trust and respect, and peaceful social coexistence. Any one who has observed developments in Latin American cities, for example, has witnessed the gradual worsening of overall living conditions and the increase of crime reflected in the erection of walls, the tightened security, the appearance of private police around the homes of wealthier classes and the gradual deterioration of social relations in those societies. Today, the same "bundle" of values and worldview also apparently feeds our dominant ethical approaches.

Surprisingly, only modern feminists question our leading social values and recognize the importance of gender issues in technology, development, and the inherent sexism in the sciences and ethics (Sen and Grown, 1985; Harding, 1986; Sherwin 1987; Mullet, 1988 and others). Feminists point out that most theories assume that moral choices are made on abstract principles, either considering the consequences of an act (the teleological principle) or are guided by the essence of an act (the deontological one). In such ethics, people are viewed as separate, independent actors and are depersonalized by an ethics in which the contextual, relational and affective aspects of their lives are disregarded. This ethics give priority to individual self-interest, ignoring the web of social relations which are the fabric of people's life. "Such view makes the social interaction an anomaly and treats it with suspicion. Most moral theories in fact seem to view social interaction in just that way. Obligations do not direct one to seek out interactions with others, to strive for cooperative arrangements, but rather to refrain from interfering excessively with the independence of some other person one might happen to bump into" says Sherwin (1987: 25).

A radically different view of ethics is proposed by modern feminists. For them, ethics based on such abstract principles and embodying such views of persons and society are unsatisfactory.

> A feminist ethics would be one that rejects the predatory conception of human interaction inherent in any theory that is essentially concerned with the separateness of persons. It would view concern and cooperation as normal, not an aberration: in such a theory, vicious competition would be viewed as a violation demanding special justification. This would differ from the approach underlying leading moral theories where pure self-interest and competition are defined normatively as "rational"... What is needed, then, is a moral theory that recognizes genuine sympathy and cooperation as valuable and encourages their development... (Sherwin, 1987: 27).

The creation of such a theory would require rethinking of the person in a social context, recognizing the mutuality between the social and the individual, rather than juxtaposing them to each other. It would view individual autonomy as freedom from oppression or domination rather than as separateness or isolation; and it would restore value to caring and to mutual support.

Such an ethical approach cannot be attained simply by theoretical reform. It calls for complex alteration and a "shift" in worldviews and consciousness. Feminists maintain that the "shift" involves acquiring a new "moral sensitivity"; experiencing an "ontological shock"; and engaging in (political) "praxis." The development of a "moral sensitivity" consists in the shedding of our moral callousness and recognizing the existence of violence, oppression, victimization and pain in our surroundings, particularly that of women (created by social change and development), no matter how unpleasant this recognition might be.

The "ontological shock" is a rejection of passive acceptance of misery and pain and a commitment to change in social conditions. It is a rejection of the appearances of naturalness and the inevitability of women's condition and of oppression and injustice in general.

"Praxis" is the outcome of collective understanding of the transformative possibilities within a given social context. It implies collective awareness and political action. "Praxis" is the shift from seeing the world as an individual moral agent to the perspective of a "we." "It is not my moral perspective that I come to understand better but the emerging moral perspective of countless others committed to changing the existing conditions in which we live" says Mullett (1988: 175). Praxis implies the idea that our perception of reality emerges from our efforts to transform it; thus thought and action are inseparably merged in "praxis." The transformative perception is a collective one, emerging from our shared attempt to understand reality. The reality which we wish to focus upon as moral agent is socially constructed: there is the possibility that reality which has not yet emerged will emerge as the result of our human efforts (Mullet, 1988). Praxis, here, doesn't deny the individual, however, it simply takes in the need for collective understanding and action for development to be accomplished.

In sum, such a moral stance could assist us in recovering our "lost human community," help reestablish social controls over technology and create development which could facilitate the emergence of cooperative, caring societies in which mutual trust and assistance are viewed as valuable and normal.

DR. E.A. CEBOTAREV is Professor of Sociology and Anthropology at the University of Guelph.

Bibliography

Baram, Michael S. "Social Control of Science and Technology" in *American Annals for the Advancement of Science*, Vol. 172, No. 3983 (Winter, 1971), pp.353–359

Bell, Daniel. *The Coming of Post-Industrial Society* (New York: Barie Books, 1973).

Berger, Peter L. *Pyramids of Sacrifice. Political Ethics and Social Change* (New York: Basic Books, 1974).

Berger, Peter L. et.al. *The Homeless Mind* (New York: Vintage Books, 1973).

Code, L.S. Mullett & Overall C. *Feminist Perspective: Philosophical Essays on Method and Morals* (Toronto: University of Toronto Press, 1988).

Crocker, David. "Moral Relativism and International Affairs," *Technos*, 8, pp.19–23.

Fals-Borda, Orlando. *Subversion and Social Change in Colombia* (New York: Columbia University Press, 1969).

Goulet, Denis. "Le Monde du Sous-Développement" Une Crise de Valeurs." Paper given at the Canadian Association of Asian Studies, Montreal (May 12) (Washington: ODC, 1975).

Goulet, Denis. *Development Ethics and Liberation Theology* (New York: Orbis Books, 1974).

Goulet, Denis. *The Cruel Choice* (New York: Atheneum, 1971a).

Goulet, Denis. "An Ethical Model for the Study of Values," *Harvard Educational Review*, Vol. 41, No. 4 (November 1971b), pp.205–227.

Jordan, F., Miranda, C., Sepulveda Sergio y Reuben W. *La Economía Campesina en la Reactivacion y Desarrollo Agropecuario* (Coronado, C.R.: IICA Série Documentos de Programas, 1989).

MacNeish, R.S., "Ancient Mesoamerican Civilization," in *Science*, Vol. 143, No. 3606 (February 1964), pp.531–537.

Mangelsdorf, P.C. et al., "Domestication of Corn" in *Science*, Vol. 143, No. 3606 (February 1964), pp.538–545.

Mullett, S. "Shifting Perspective: A New Approach to Ethics" in Code et al. *op.cit.*

Sherwin, S. "A Feminist Approach to Ethics" in RFR/DRF, *Women and Philosophy*, Vol. 16, No. 3, pp.25–28.

UNIT III
SUSTAINABLE RESOURCES

8   *Terisa E. Turner*

Ethics and Energy Technology

As a political economist who has lived and worked in many countries, especially in the Third World, I have had one foot in the policy realm, notably through the United Nations, and the other foot in academia. The methodology used here to consider ethical dimensions of energy technology are fourfold. First, to define the terms political economy, ethics, energy and technology. Second, to examine the history of action in the energy sector from an ethical point of view. Third, to consider what action is necessary if the technology for energy production and distribution is to serve ethical ends as defined by the majority of the world's population. Fourth, and in conclusion, to suggest actions which are possible now.

Definitions

> In an advanced industrial society, capitalism organizes the working class by putting them together in huge factories, by putting them all to live in the most convenient spots to get to work early in the morning. So that the working class is united, it is disciplined and it is organized by the very mechanism of capitalist production itself; and the more progressive capitalist production is, the more it unites those who are destined to be its grave-diggers.[1]

Political economy is the analysis of the formation and interaction of social classes historically and on a world scale. Because the analysis here is a political economy analysis it centers on relations among people as organized into social classes. It is by necessity an international analysis, recognizing that certainly since 1492 when Columbus unified the world market, we have been living in a globalized society.

Technology is deeply involved in the formation of social classes and the interaction or struggle among them. Machines were invented and established in ever larger production units as a result of wealth secured through trade, especially the triangular trade between Europe, Africa and the new world in the 1600s and 1700s. This trade demanded more production. The companies which survived and flourished were those able to buy, innovate and use production equipment which incorporated ever larger numbers of people, directly or indirectly. In short, budding capitalists had to introduce new technologies in order to compete with rival capitalists.

---

[1] C.L.R. James, *Modern Politics*, (Detroit: Facing Reality, 1960 and 1973), p.53.

At the same time, slaves and workers resisted exploitation. This resistance motivated capitalists to replace them with "dead labour," that is to say, with technology. Of course "dead labour" or the accumulated work of everyone who contributed to the making of the technology could only be made to "come alive" with energy. Consequently, the capitalist who had replaced living with dead labour became increasingly dependent upon energy and energy workers, in order to make technology function.

Energy—the ability to do work—has a very special and strategic part to play in the modern economy. In a highly original essay, "Why does capital need energy?" Renfrew Christie explains two dimensions of this strategic preeminence.[1]

First, energy is a commodity like any other item that is produced, marketed and consumed. Produced in oil and energy corporations, it is guaranteed to generate high profits especially if controlled by a monopoly or by a few firms operating like a monopoly (an oligopoly). The highest proportion of commercial energy consumed worldwide over the past two hundred years has been supplied by coal and petroleum, both of which are especially susceptible to monopoly.

Exxon, the world's largest oil company, was founded through Rockefeller's successful struggle to monopolize oil transportation in the late 1900s. The price of oil can be fixed much higher than the production cost because oil is found in a few reservoirs in specific locations which can be controlled through political initiatives. Indeed, the two World Wars of this century were to a large extent oil and resource wars: the major oil companies, through their home governments, fought for control of the geographical areas rich in oil. The oil industry is highly susceptible to near monopoly profits, whether from control of the reservoirs, the transport system, or the consumer outlets.

Oil companies have extended their control by buying up or developing other types of energy, notably coal and nuclear. Consequently, private and state corporations in the energy sector have expanded and now constitute the largest, most dynamic and most international of all organizations which history has hitherto produced. This means that oil workers and oil technology (and technology and labour in other types of energy) are also international and can only function on a sophisticated, global level.

The second reason for the strategic importance of energy is its special capacity to make machines function. It is essential for the use of all technology. But the real strategic importance derives from the part played by machines, i.e. "gadget" technologies in the interaction among and between capitalists, workers, and citizens in general.

Improved technology is one route to higher productivity and hence to successful inter-capitalist competition. But more important, technology can replace workers who through various forms of resistance to exploitation, challenge the employer's ability to control the production system so as to maximize long term profits for their own benefit. And since only energy can give the capitalist the ability to out-compete other capitalists or lay-off striking workers in favour of

---

Renfrew Christie, "Why Does Capital Need Energy? " in P. Nore and T. Turner, *Oil and Class Struggle*, (London: Zed, 1980.), pp.10–25.

automation, energy workers have immense potential power. If they stop producing oil or coal, stockpiles are exhausted in a few weeks and technology stops. We only have to think of the blackouts in New York in the 1970s or the three-day week in the United Kingdom in 1974 as a result of the coal miners' strike and oil embargo by the Organization of Arab Petroleum Exporting Countries (OAPEC).

This tremendous social power in the hands of energy workers has of course motivated oil and energy capitalists to automate. Here nuclear energy has been their key counter measure. Another counter measure is for oil capital to find and produce oil from national as opposed to foreign territories. Thus we have seen the expansion of expensive, environmentally sensitive exploitation in the Arctic north and in the North Sea. Capital's counter measures have proliferated energy technologies which damage the ecological balance and this has sparked growing public mobilization in favour of a new energy ethics. In sum, the special status of energy in the modern world is based on its susceptibility to monopoly profits and on its strategic character as the force bringing technology alive. The high profits have been translated into corporate empires which unite an international workforce and the consuming public. Consumers include other corporations, the military and citizens, both urban and rural. The unity is the basis for the ethical turmoil now evident in the energy sector.

Technology in the energy sector unites large numbers of people in local, regional and most important, in international networks. Because we are required by the technology to work together, we daily break down divisions among us based on gender, race, age, nationality and other differences. We become socialized as a unit and it is this working unity that impels us to be planners, responsible members of a collective whole who can improve the operation of the energy system. The technology has developed, under the impetus of the profit motive, to the point that all the world's people have been drawn into a single net. Individuals consequently have in front of us, international issues, challenges, operations, products and responsibilities which can be managed or addressed only in common.

In short, the technology of capitalism has required of workers and citizens the kind of interaction which has stimulated democratic practice. But this democratic practice is often constrained by the presence of elite or bureaucratic control through a small group of owners and managers at the top of the hierarchy of the private firm or the state corporation.

Ethics are values embodied in ultimate objectives. The fundamental ethical principle informing this discussion is the positive value of life. The basic question then is whether any activity or product supports all life or whether it results in environmental and human death. At the center of this conception is universal life, that is the well-being of the world's ecological system and well-being of all people, born now and in the future.

The formation and interaction of social classes over the last few centuries has posited two opposing ethics. First are the ethics of capital. In practice, the process of realizing the goals of the modern firm is accelerating ecological degradation and threatening the well-being of the vast majority of the world's people now and in the future. In theory, capital and the profit motive are geared to utilitarianism: the greatest good for the greatest number. But this does not work. Consumerism and the accumulation of material goods is not the highest human value. And universal equity renders inadequate notions of "the greatest number."

The second kind of ethics to evolve with the development of the modern system champions life as its highest goal. An inevitable concomitant of economic expansion is the growth of democratic sentiment and democratic practice at the point of production. It is vital to note that production takes place at work and at home. Products and services are produced in both places, and democratic practice is transforming the relationships into which we enter with our colleagues, our spouses and families as well as in our communities.

This evolving morality which champions all life is not a psychological, religious or voluntaristic phenomenon. It is a material force undivorceable from modern technology. It is a result of the development of the political economy. In particular, the ethics which support all human life have emerged from the development of globalizing technology. We are interdependent in our work and in our survival. In order to work in a rewarding and safe manner, and in order to maximize the human content of our existence, we must recognize the need for a global equity which addresses the needs of the worst off first. Specifically, the ethics which support life in the energy sector encompass at least three goals. These goals have to do with equity, technology and physical resources. First, there must be equality of access to energy by all the world's people. Second, the ways in which we produce and transport energy must be safe and sustainable. And third, we should consume only as much energy from non-renewable sources as will leave sufficient resources form coming generations. Clearly, the profit motive cannot be the goal if these principles are to be realized.

A Process For Change

Major energy corporations have made change both necessary and possible. the change has to do with goals. Is the energy system to continue to be guided by the goal of maximizing profits or is it going to promote global social well-being? A change in goals is necessary because millions now recognize the incompatibility of profit maximization and broad social well-being. Major energy corporations have pursued profitability to the point of endangering the planet. There have been several decades of energy wars and tremendous suffering as a result of the strategies of major oil corporations. Pollution and its future escalation add to the popular convictions about the need for change in goals and what this change implies for new organizational and accountability dynamics.

By the same token, energy workers and citizens are both mobilized and impelled by capital to change the ethical goals of energy activity. Capital has made it possible and necessary to act. In general, there are two types of effective action. Change may be brought about through the exercise of either consumption boycotts or strikes. Under capitalism, the two forms of social power which the exploited population has at its disposal are the refusal to consume and the refusal to produce. Inherent in both are the impetus to organize alternative ways of securing essential consumption goods, and to resume or substitute production, guided by democratic goals and dynamics of social organization. Frequently, as in South Africa today, strikes or "stay-at-homes" and consumer boycotts are used simultaneously.

A New Morality

Some of the ways in which energy workers[1] and energy consumers have engaged in life-supporting ethical practice to re-orient the morality of the world energy system are through direct actions, such as strikes and citizen action, oil embargoes, and employee vigilance.

Direct Action: Strikes

The Iranian oil workers' strike in 1978–79[2] is a most dramatic instance of oil workers defining and enforcing a new morality for the energy sector. They shut down the world's second largest oil export operation, involving production of some six million barrels a day. Combined with a national uprising, their action forced the repressive Shah to flee. They stopped exporting oil to South Africa which was getting 90 per cent of its supplies from the Shah's Iran. This international initiative delivered a severe shock to the apartheid regime. It probably dealt the death knell to Ian Smith's white minority rule in Rhodesia and it strengthened the United Nations campaign for an oil boycott against South Africa and in favour of Namibian independence.

Citizen Action: No Nukes

The most powerful citizen's movements have been against nuclear reactors for electricity generation. Two cases are prominent in the late 1980s. The U.S.-based Clamshell Alliance has mobilized again against the restarting of the New Hampshire, Seabrook nuclear plant. In June 1989 almost 1,000 protestors were arrested at the plant site, and mobilization is growing. Another element in this campaign is citizen decisions to designate cities and towns "nuclear free zones." Second, an historic vote in a California community in June 1989 determined that a nuclear reactor should be mothballed rather than continue to generate electricity.

These actions along with thousands of others like them have forced oil and energy corporations to "internalize" the costs of pollution, waste disposal, evacuation plans and environmental measures. Hence, the costs of providing nuclear generated electricity have risen, the returns have been reduced and banks are increasingly reluctant to lend funds for nuclear reactor construction. This reality

---

[1] Broadly speaking, energy workers include all men and women, whether waged or unwaged, who produce, gather, process and transport any type of energy. We can also include women and others working in the household providing services for members of the family who are employed in the energy production system. Labour essential to the strategic energy industry derives directly from waged workers and indirectly from those (usually unwaged "homemakers") who produce the labour power of waged workers. Thus struggles by energy workers include actions by those (mainly men) who produce and refine oil, but also actions by those (mainly women) who produce and refine those who produce and refine oil.

[2] Terisa E. Turner, "Iranian Oilworkers in the 1978–79 Revolution," in P. Nore and T. Turner, (eds.) *Oil and Class Struggle*, (London: Zed, 1980), pp.272–292.

combined with Three Mile Island, Chernobyl and the increased danger of meltdown in ageing plants has dealt the nuclear industry a blow from which it may never recover. Citizen action has put the nuclear industry on hold. To the extent that nuclear energy and weapons constitute one industry, citizen action has also promoted détente, disarmament and reduced the danger of nuclear holocaust.

Ecological Survival

Citizen action against energy-related pollution and ecological danger have also made an impact. Organizations such as Green Peace have called for a halt in licensing offshore areas to petroleum corporations in the wake of the 1989 Exxon oil spill in Alaska. A global campaign to halt clearing of rainforests has blocked the development of the Zingu hydroelectric dam in Brazil. One case study of this campaign shows how workers in the world's largest non-military computer communications system, Digital, use their technology to mobilize against the World Bank's attempt to lend Brazil's government funds for the dam[1]. The Rainforest Action Coalition now has international scope and has organized boycotts of fast food outlets which buy beef from corporations engaged in agro-industry on land from which the forests have recently been cleared.

The Rationality of Indigenous Peoples

The citizen actions cited above emphasize the use of global communications and networking techniques typical of industrialized societies. However, rural, Third World peasant and indigenous peoples also affirm life-supporting ethics in the energy sphere. Resistance to new cooking technologies and new home heating systems illustrate the rationality and morality of those who constitute the majority of the world's population.

A large proportion of the energy consumed in the Third World is biomass, usually in the form of fuel wood gathered by women and children. Women use fuel wood mainly for cooking. Peasant cultures have been attacked for over gathering of fuel wood which is said to be responsible for deforestation and the extension of the desert. However, deeper analysis and historical investigation suggest that mining companies, the timber and agro-industry, and other corporate activity have played a larger part in the elimination of forest cover. The rationality of the small farmer or peasant in land use has been reaffirmed. The attack on peasant energy practices is frequently a prelude to marketing efforts by foreign or state interests seeking to promote more "efficient" though not necessarily cost effective cooking stoves and other technologies. These technologies may indeed reduce waste and promote energy efficiency, but they cost money and hence are a motivation for the peasant to enter more deeply into the cash economy. This usually reduces the peasant woman's scope for independent survival, integrating her further as it does into wage labour relations. This is part of the process of alienating her from the land and therefore from the source of food and the

---

[1]
David Caputo, "The Rainforest, The Dead and Digital: Using Worldwide Communications Networks To Encourage Planetary Survival," in Terisa E. Turner. et. al.(ed), *Revolutionary Popular Culture*, (New York: International Oil Working Group, 1989), pp.139–158.

possibility of feeding her children. Urban poverty and malnutrition follow close behind.

Oil Embargoes

The oil embargo against South Africa is worth highlighting. Like Japan, South Africa has no oil of its own. Without oil, apartheid's police and military could not repress the majority black population. Workers in the energy system have extended the Iranian oil workers' initiative to stop oil to South Africa. This must be seen as part of a tendency for oil workers to directly control and operate the world market in petroleum, thus bypassing and disempowering the traders and multinational oil corporations.

Countless localized actions by tanker workers, dock and terminal workers, as well as production and refinery personnel have blocked specific shipments of oil to South Africa.[1] The anti-apartheid struggle within South Africa has stimulated international cooperation among oil workers. The national seamen's unions of the United Kingdom, Denmark and Australia established the Maritime Unions Against Apartheid in 1984. The goals of this international network include receiving information from seamen and terminal operators about which vessels or companies engage in sanctions busting, and coordinating international action against them.

It has proved difficult for a multinational oil corporation to operate both in South Africa and in oil-rich societies where oil workers and other citizens are committed to ending apartheid. Mobil's 1989 withdrawal from South Africa was influenced by Nigerian oil workers' resistance to the Nigerian government allowing Mobil to expand operations in Nigeria's offshore areas.[2] Mobil's pullout was also the result of U.S. Congressional action, in response to workers' and citizens' campaigns, which denied U.S. firms the right to subtract taxes paid to the apartheid regime from taxes owed to the U.S. government.

It is difficult to assess the degree to which the oil embargo is an effective weapon against apartheid. It is even more difficult to quantify the degree of unity in practice among oil workers, worldwide, in embargo enforcement. However, the trend is toward greater unity and capacity to control the movement of oil in the world market.

---

[1] Terisa E. Turner, *Trade Union Action to Stop Oil to South Africa*, (Aba, Nigeria: Sebachien for the Organization of African Trade Union Unity and the Publication Committee of the University of Port Harcourt, 1985).

[2] Terisa E. Turner, "Oil workers and the Oil Bust in Nigeria," *Africa Today*, (Denver: University of Colorado, 4th Quarter 1989), pp.33–50 and "Sanctions and Energy: The Withdrawal of Mobil Oil From South Africa," (African Studies Association 32nd Annual Meeting Paper, (Atlanta, Georgia, November 2 to 5, 1989).

Vigilance Against Pollution

Finally, in terms of employee vigilance, employees of energy corporations have begun to disclose data about health, safety and ecologically hazardous practices on the part of management. Exploitation of energy workers causes dangers in the workplace. Conditions are typically poor and rather than invest in safety measures, corporations retain funds for profits or further capital investment. Especially in oil exploration, a bogus "macho" is promoted to encourage workers to brave dangers and work long hours. These conditions breed accidents that kill and pollute. Many examples of oil workers acting against pollution may be cited. In Trinidad and Tobago, contract workers for Standard Oil of Indiana (Amoco) took clandestine photographs of toxic fluid which was being discharged directly into the Atlantic Ocean in a fishing and tourist area off the south east coast of Trinidad. The discharge pipe was situated in a no-go zone policed by Amoco's security.[1]

Members of the Oilfields Workers' Trade Union in Trinidad drew attention to Texaco's on land pipelines which were leaking oil. The pipes were old and in need of replacement, but Texaco ordered workers to clamp strips of rubber around the leaky pipes to temporarily curb the flow of petroleum. Workers photographed these pipes and raised the issue of Texaco's pollution at a national enquiry into foreign control of the country's oil industry in 1979. In the mid 1980s Texaco sold out most of its holdings (but lucrative offshore production areas) to the government which is reluctant to clean up the pollution and replace hundreds of miles of aged pipes.

An Ethical Agenda For Energy Development

What change is necessary? What are the elements of an ethical agenda for the use of energy technologies that will create a humane and sustainable future? Of particular significance are answers available from two sources. First, what do actors in the energy system demand, especially when they are in the process of seeking change? Second, what have specialized conferences, resource people and studies recommended?

Energy workers and citizens, organized in production and living situations by modern technology, have put on the agenda a wide range of demands for change in the energy sector. Mention has been made of energy conservation, the drive to close down nuclear reactors, the call for an end to pollution including acid rain, opposition to large-scale hydroelectric projects, the tendency toward worker control at all stages of the energy industry and an end to offshore licensing for oil exploration.

Demands made by workers and citizens are especially important because of the social power at the disposal of these interests. Workers have the potential capacity to enforce their demands and to implement them. Citizens, using a wide variety of resources including the ballot and consumer boycotts, have a degree of implementing power. Consequently demands which arise in the process of change

---

[1] Donna Coombs, "Women and Recession in an Oil Exporting Society: The Case of Trinidad and Tobago," in Terisa E. Turner et.al., (eds.), *Revolutionary Popular Culture*, (New York: International Oil Working Group, 1989).

are constituent elements of popular energy planning. And such planning is informed by in-depth knowledge of the problems and potentials. It is compelling because it is practical. Such planning puts the well-being of people before profits. While coordination is essential, there is no need for corporate or state involvement in peoples' energy planning. A example of popular planning in the energy sector is provided by public employees in Nigeria's electricity authority. Frustrated with endemic power outages technicians formulated in 1983 a repair and maintenance plan which was resisted by senior officials. Nevertheless, the conception of how to make affordable, stable electric service more widely available has been established.

The second source of guidance for the ethical transformation of the energy system is specialized analysis. An astonishing amount of technical data has been generated and published since the energy crisis of 1973.

It is evident that solar technology now exists and can be much more widely disseminated with public sector support. Solar is vastly superior to coal and petroleum from the ecological point of view. And petroleum, a finite resource, is too valuable to burn. Many resource people advocate decentralized and integrated energy supply networks which would be appropriate for certain regions. Public transport systems are dramatically less energy intensive than are systems based on the automobile. Trains are cheaper than trucks. Bicycle transport has much to recommend it. There is widespread agreement that nuclear energy is prohibitively expensive if all the costs, including the cost of waste management and emergency preparedness, are taken into account. With nuclear energy and all other energy sources, the full cost (including technologies) should be considered in calculating socio-economic impact. In order to end the proliferation of nuclear reactors and weapons to the Third World, it is essential for the industrial world to engage in a phased shut down.

Nairobi's 1982 United Nations conference on new and renewable sources of energy centralized vast quantities of data on energy and technologies available especially for the Third World. In virtually every subsector of the energy system, specialized knowledge exists. Answers have been posed, but more political capacity to implement solutions is necessary. Nevertheless, the definition of an agenda for a humane energy future has made remarkable technical progress. The current challenges are rooted in the realm of political economy.

Conclusions

The evidence of recent decades suggests that tremendous advances toward instituting humane, sustainable energy systems have been made by energy workers and consumers, especially citizen consumers. To the extent that governments, institutions and resource people accept this evidence as valid, they will lend support to further developing the creative capacities of workers and citizens. The broad objectives include encouraging worker vigilance about dangers in the energy production-consumption cycle; affirming grassroots planning initiatives, spreading the message through formal and public education that ecological sustainability is the world society's highest priority, along with building confidence in people's abilities to solve problems creatively. In short, the broad policy guidelines should promote democratic practice by workers on the job and citizens in the community.

What types of assistance can educators, policy makers, foundations and institutions provide to citizens and workers?

To support citizens in building a sustainable, humane energy future; policy makers can:

- hold more conferences similar to the 1989 international meeting on "Ethics and Technology" in Guelph, Canada. Especially valuable are follow-up conferences every three to five years, such as were organized around women and gender relations by the United Nations. Such sequential conferences allow for interim local and regional organizing, as well as for the testing of solutions in practice.
- provide financial support for information and action campaigns by citizens seeking to educate and poll public opinion regarding, for example, the continued operation of a nuclear facility. Such support would offset the tremendous financial advantage that utility corporations have over citizen groups in campaigns.
- finance rallies and demonstrations such as the historic anti-nuclear demonstration which attracted nearly a million people to New York city in 1982.
- subsidize conversion to solar energy through tax breaks and other means. Government policy has relied on petroleum tax as a source of income generation to the point that there is a vested interest on the part of many states to expand oil use rather than provide tax relief to individuals and organizations interested in safe, renewable alternatives.
- bring together citizens from various communities, nationally and internationally, to share experiences in fighting pollution from a particular source. Many waste disposal problems must be addressed on an international basis. One locale cannot "solve" waste disposal by exporting it to a poor country, the government of which consciously or inadvertently allows for toxic dumping. This merely globalizes life-threatening pollution at an ever-accelerating rate.
- reorient education at all levels, and especially in the sciences, to reward critical perspectives on technology and software. Students must be stimulated to discover whether assignments support ecologically degrading or life-supporting solutions. To the extent that education is organized and financed by corporate management, it will, with few exceptions, serve short-term profit objectives. Consequently funds from non-corporate sources (governments and foundations) should be earmarked for critical education.

To support workers in building a sustainable, humane energy future policy makers can:

- promote workplace democracy in both public and private energy corporations. Ideas and practices which reduce environmental degradation and workplace danger should be encouraged through newsletters, meetings, public recognition and other means. Democratic

practice within unions at the local level, and throughout the organization is a value which requires much more support.
- adopt and disseminate the principle that energy workers should be politically engaged in the work process and in league with citizen groups.
- strengthen international worker coordination.
- fund the use of computer networks for the establishment of systems of reporting and communication among energy workers worldwide. Such systems could help prevent environmental disasters such as oil spills, and emergency relief could more efficiently be mobilized.
- fund more research on all forms of non-polluting, renewable energy sources and their technologies.
- promote participatory research on the social and political economy circumstances under which existing new and renewable energies can be introduced.
- expand funding for research on methods of restoring environments and isolating existing nuclear and other dangerous wastes.
- support conversion of nuclear facilities to more benign production, and the promotion of wide ranging campaigns for conversion, including training of workers.
- exame obstacles to self-organization in the community and workplace with a view to overcoming divisions among people based on sex, race, national origin and other differences.

In conclusion, those who recognize the need for radical change in ethical practices have grounds for optimism. Technology has united the world. It has generated both imperatives and capacities to reorient society from profit maximization and war to a way of life which is egalitarian, humane and sustainable. Because of the vested interests of social classes, successful reorientation requires struggle. It is a challenge worthy of a life time commitment. The future of our world literally depends upon our taking up this struggle.

NOTE: The philosophy underpinning the ideas presented here comes very much from the writing and action of Trinidadian revolutionary intellectual, C.L.R. James. This remarkably creative Marxist died at the age of 88 on 31 May 1989 in Brixton, London. I had worked with him since 1968. I went to Trinidad where the oil union buried C.L.R. James in his village, Tunapuna. Dozens of eulogies resonate in my head. Novelist George Lamming insists that C.L.R. James was an evangelist, celebrating the capacities of ordinary people to re-order the world in accord with an all-encompassing definition of humanity. Our capacities, James insisted, come from the organization among us required and made possible by technology. It is this spirit that moves me as I write now. I include references from James' books and a selection for further reading at the end.

DR. T.E. TURNER is a Canadian energy economist and co-director of the International Oil Working Group, a non-governmental organization registered with the United Nations in New York; Associate Professor of Social Thought and Political Economy, Machmer E–27, University of Massachusetts, Amherst. Comments on this discussion would be welcome. Please send them to IOWG, P.O. Box 1410, Cathedral Station, New York, New York, 10025, USA. Appreciation is due to the following people for their assistance with this draft: Joe Young, Rodrick Thurton, Leigh Brownhill, Timothy Belknap, Jason Murray, Ralph Reed and Brian Bannon.

Further Reading

Agarwal, Bina, *Cold Hearths and Barren Slopes* (London: Zed, 1986).

Bott, Robert, David Brooks and John Robinson, *Life After Oil: A Renewable Energy Policy for Canada* (Edmonton: Hurtig and Friends of the Earth, 1983).

Energy 2000: A Global Strategy for Sustainable Development, Report to the World Commission on Environment and Development (London: Zed, 1987).

James, C.L.R. *The Future in the Present*, Selected Writings, Volume one, (1977). *Spheres of Existence*, Volume Two, (1979). *At The Rendezvous of Victory*, Volume Three (London: Allison and Busby, 1979).

Martinez-Alier, Juan, *Energy and Ecology* (Oxford: Basil Blackwell, 1988).

Nore, Petter and Terisa Turner, (eds.), *Oil and Class Struggle* (London: Zed, 1980).

Turner, Terisa E. et al., (eds.), *Revolutionary Popular Culture* (New York: International Oil Working Group, 1989).

Frank Hurnik and Hugh Lehman

Technology and Choice in Agriculture

In the recent past, the primary objectives of agriculturalists have been both to increase agricultural outputs and to reduce the drudgery required to do so. In animal agriculture, these goals have been accomplished through methods which include improved nutrition, use of growth promotants, scientifically improved breeds, intensive confinement of animals and mechanization of many husbandry chores. In plant agriculture, these goals have been accomplished through the use of synthetic fertilizers, herbicides, pesticides, genetically improved varieties adapted to environments that previously had been less favourable, and again, through the use of larger and more powerful machinery. The high standard of living which we in the industrialized world enjoy owes a great deal to the technology resulting from the application of scientific knowledge developed by agricultural scientists. Similarly, the improvements in human nutrition which have occurred in parts of the developing world also derive from applications of scientific knowledge in food production.

The above objectives, increased output and reduced drudgery, are themselves justifiable as means to laudable ends. To the extent that these goals have been achieved, an increasing number of people have led longer, and probably, happier lives. If one looks at this result within the perspective of a teleological ethical theory, this is clearly an improvement. The accomplishment of these goals is also justified on deontological grounds. In the industrialized world, since the end of the World War II, we have moved closer to the ideal of treating every person as a free moral being capable of directing his or her own life. Without the abundance made possible in part by modern agriculture, it is unlikely that we would have achieved as much.

Scientists who have worked all their lives to devise methods to increase production and reduce drudgery see their task as still unfinished. There continues to be people who do not have enough nourishing food. Further, increasing population and a deteriorating environment may undermine the improvements achieved thus far. Using modern scientific methods, these scientists try to develop new cultivars with higher yields, to devise methods to increase milk production, etc. However, others, including biologists, philosophers and social scientists have become alarmed. Concerns have been expressed in four areas: protection of the environment, human health, preservation of individual liberty and well-being, and animal welfare. The very same ethical principles which buttressed the arguments justifying our efforts to increase production and reduce drudgery may also enable the questioning of agricultural practices. The reasoning which gives rise to these concerns is at least good enough to warrant saying that scientists, agriculturalists,

producers, philosophers, politicians and others should take a long hard look at the problem areas. The criticisms should be carefully evaluated and, where necessary, public policies may need to be changed.

Criticism of modern agricultural technology has appeared on four fronts. In the first place, modern agricultural methods are perceived as contributing to the destruction of the environment which is essential for the survival of both human and other forms of life on Earth. The very methods which have led to increased productivity have simultaneously led to a deteriorating environment. Increased productivity has been developed through the use of large agricultural machinery and agricultural chemicals. To accommodate the large equipment, framers have to plow long straight lines. This contributes to loss of topsoil due to water erosion. Windbreaks have been cut down to make larger fields and this contributes to loss of topsoil due to wind erosion. Marshes have been drained and fields plowed right to the edge of rivers or streams. This has contributed to the elimination of varieties of species from our environments. Again, power for the machinery is derived from combustion of oil and this contributes carbon to the atmosphere and so may exacerbate the so-called "Greenhouse Effect." While considering pollution, we must also mention that the use of nitrogen compounds and other substances in agriculture has led to water contamination. The result is eutrophication of lakes and pollution of human drinking water.

Secondly, intensive methods in both plant and animal agriculture are perceived as dangerous to human health. Of primary concern in this regard is the widespread use of herbicides, pesticides, growth promotants, etc. Use of such products is a danger to those who apply them. Moreover, there is danger to those people who consume the agricultural products which have been treated with such substances. Respected medical journals have cited strong evidence of human infection resulting in part from the use of antibiotics in animal feed. Further, there is increasing concern both about residues of pesticides etc. from substances used to grow food products and also about other substances added to food in the course of processing and packaging.

Thirdly, some people are concerned that recent changes in agricultural technology will cause changes to social and economic structures which in turn may weaken democratic government and the protection of individual welfare. As a result of the high costs of certain forms of technology, such technologies may be accessible only to large agricultural corporations with sufficient capital resources to bear the costs. As an example, consider the new forms of food processing technology which involve irradiation of food. Here, consideration of safety as well as costs suggest that this technology will only be used by large corporations. Again, with the advent of genetic manipulations, corporations may be given the legal right to patent new life forms. Smaller firms may not be able to compete successfully in areas where these forms of technology are applied. If, in shaping our future we wish to preserve a high degree of decentralized power as a means of preserving individual autonomy and welfare, we may have to devise methods to insure that opportunities for small scale production systems are maintained.

Last but not least, a growing number of people perceive intensive animal agriculture as involving many cruel abuses of animals. A huge number of animals in intensive production systems have to live in isolated and very confined spaces. In addition, there is often crowding of many animals, restriction of diets in ways incompatible with animal health, deprivation of light and no freedom to associate with conspecifics.

In discussing the four areas of concern about technology we have already made reference to one of the *newest* forms of technology, namely manipulation of the genetic structure of organisms. This form of biotechnology has been the cause of increasing concern both with respect to human health and with respect to the state of the environment. The new technology is based on knowledge of the genetic bases of phenotypic traits and involves inserting genes from some individuals into the genetic material of others. Such transplantation of genes is not limited by species boundaries. Whereas in the past geneticists were able to develop new cultivars, for example of corn through selective breeding, now, through the manipulation of genes, scientists may be able to achieve comparable increases in a small fraction of the time. Similarly, the new technology holds out the promise of plants that have increased resistance to frost and to pests—in other words, plants which can thrive in a wider range of environments. Transplantation of genes has been used to create new forms of bacteria and also new forms of animals. Such technology could contribute to the development of more sustainable forms of agriculture. Conceivably, through such methods, many plants could be endowed with nitrogen fixing capability thus reducing our dependence on nitrogen fertilizer which currently requires large inputs of energy in its production. Such a development would not only lessen our dependence on shrinking energy reserves but also reduce nitrogen contamination of our lakes and rivers.

While such genetic technology holds great promise of benefits for human beings, there are also risks. The primary concern is that a genetically engineered organism will escape from the control of its creators. Such a new organism could conceivably cause profound environmental changes—changes which might not be beneficial to people or other creatures. The creation of new forms of life, especially through the transplantation of genes across species boundaries, poses a challenge to certain deeply felt religious beliefs. The creation stories in the first chapters of Genesis are taken by some as implying that species boundaries ought not to be breached.

Clearly, we have choices open to us. We have choices to make as to how we confront our changing environment. We can continue with business as usual. Many people think that if we follow this course the result will be disastrous—perhaps even the extinction of the human species. Alternatively, we can investigate the great complexities involved in the ecosystems within which we exist. Such a course promises the ability to deploy different kinds of agri-technology which are sustainable in the long-run.

We can continue to employ large amounts of herbicides, pesticides etc. to obtain high productivity or alternatively we can reduce our dependence on such substances. If we choose to do the latter, there are further choices open to us. We could decide to accept lower productivity levels. However, there may be ways of reducing or eliminating the use of these substances without reducing productivity. We could attempt to develop new varieties of crops which are resistant to pests. We can attempt to develop animals which are more productive even without the use of antibiotics or other substances to stimulate growth, milk production, etc. Still another choice is to maintain productivity using methods which are more labour intensive.

We can continue to intensify methods of agricultural production. Many producers of animal products favour even further reductions in space, greater crowding, etc. for animals. Alternatively, we can adopt methods of animal production which provide animals with more space and, in general, an improved quality of life.

Among both supporters and opponents of the use of modern technology, we find that the choices open to us are often presented rather simplistically. That is, we can either continue to use modern technology or we can abandon it. Both groups appeal to this claim in support of their perspectives. Each group argues by way of a dilemma.

The supporters of scientific technology argue: Either we can retain scientific technology or we can abandon it. If we abandon it, our lives, as in earlier times, will be "nasty, brutish and short." If we retain it, we will continue to progress in improving individual welfare and dignity. For them, the choice is obvious—either increased welfare and dignity—or lives which are nasty, brutish and short. Similarly, the opponents of scientific technology argue: Either we retain scientific technology or we can abandon it. However, if we retain it, we will suffer and bring on disaster through the destruction of our environment or our democratic liberties. If we abandon it, we will avoid the complex dangers brought on by modern technology so that human beings can again lead happy lives.

Both of the above dilemmas are open to criticism on several counts. Here we shall criticize only the premise which is common to them both. In each argument, we are presented with a false dichotomy. Clearly, to argue that we have only two choices, namely either to retain or abandon technology, is to accept a fallacious premise. As is indicated above, we can retain some technologies and abandon others, and, the way in which a technology is deployed can also be influenced through our choices. We are not in the position of having to choose between the "brave new world" and life under conditions that prevailed in the stone age or before.

Clearly, the choices we make with regard to the above issues should be determined by democratic processes. However, the issues are complex. To arrive at a reasonable basis for choice, we must find a rational way to integrate both factual as well as normative judgments. Scientific *and* practical considerations must be taken into account. To this end, academics, business people, and people in government must overcome what we may call "the ostrich syndrome," that is, the disposition to keep our heads firmly planted in the sand so as not to see the problems which confront us. Too often, scientists, business people, politicians and others give way to the disposition to ignore implications of what they do and so fail to exercise responsibility with respect to the consequences of their actions.

To succeed in the effort to arrive at rational solutions in response to the questions which confront us, requires imagination and critical analysis on the part of people from many areas of life. This in turn requires overcoming long-standing tendencies which have led people in these different areas to distrust each other. It is to be hoped that we have the maturity to carry out programmes which will preserve a high quality of life on Earth.

DR. F. HURNIK is Professor of Animal and Poultry Science at the University of Guelph.

DR. H. LEHMAN is Professor of Philosophy at the University of Guelph.

Reprinted with Permission from the *Journal of Agricultural Ethics.*

Further Reading

Animal Rights

Regan, Tom and Singer, Peter. *Animal Rights and Human Obligations* (Englewood Cliffs: Prentice-Hall, 1976).

Sapontzis, S.F. *Morals, Reason and Animals* (Philadelphia: Temple University Press, 1987).

Environmental Ethics

Rolston, Holmes. *Environmental Ethics, Duties to and Values in the Natural World*, III. (Philadelphia: Temple University Press, 1986).

Sagoff, Mark. *The Economy of the Earth: Philosophy, Law and the Environment* (Cambridge: Cambridge University Press, 1988).

Journals

The Journal of Agricultural Ethics

Environmental Ethics

Agriculture and Human Values

UNIT IV
ECONOMIC
EFFICIENCY

10 *Daphne S. Taylor and Truman P. Phillips*

Economics and Ethics of Technological Change

If necessity is the mother of invention, then economics can make legitimate claim of part parentage of technological innovation. Economics plays a dual role in both signalling what type of inventions are needed, and what type of inventions will be adopted. Economics also offers an analytical framework from which the ethical and political implications arising from technological change can be expressed in logical terms, understood and eventually altered. The term "economics," as used here, has a double meaning: an activity dealing with the creation and distribution of goods and services and a discipline which studies such activities. Although it is common to hear that economics is completely "value-free," a deeper understanding of economics, both as a process and as a discipline, indicates that it is often based on value preferences. As John Kenneth Galbraith reminds us: " ... economic ideas are always and intimately a product of their own time and place; they cannot be seen apart from the world they interpret." [1]

On the one hand, economic systems, as concrete forms of production and distribution reflect the values of the community and/or its dominant groups. On the other hand, economic analysis, beyond the logic of its formulations, rests upon normative assumptions. In this sense, a complex triangular relationship exists between values and economics, economics and technology, and technology and values. We will examine the first two relationships below. An examination of values and technology may be found in other articles.

The Relationship of Economics and Values

In all economic systems, market and non-market forces influence the allocation of resources, the choice of technology and the composition and distribution of goods and services. Within the marketplace, forces of supply and demand determine prices. Prices, in turn, coordinate the decisions of producers and consumers and therefore influence the allocation of resources, the choices in technologies, and the resulting composition and eventual distribution of goods and services. The role of social or political systems (non-market forces) is to determine if such allocations, compositions and distribution of goods meet the values of society. If they do not, action in the form of policy is warranted which intervene in the economic system to achieve alternative outcomes.

John Kenneth Galbraith, *Economics in Perspective: A Critical History*, (Boston: Houghton Mifflin Co., 1987), p.1.

Economic systems and tools reflect societal values. Society, through its decision-making mechanisms, decides whether the production and distribution of goods and services is coordinated by market forces or is centrally planned. Economics[1] per se does not determine social values nor does it claim that a particular social state is better than another. These are matters of moral or political philosophy. The role of economics is simply to identify the circumstances from which values judgements and social objectives are determined and given those circumstances to suggest the appropriate policy instruments (or means) which will achieve desired objectives. Thus society, or influential groups within it, determine social norms and collective goals to be accomplished through economic processes. The discipline of economics only provides a methodology to assess the probable consequences of such a course or alternative courses.

The Relationship of Economics and Technological Change

Technology, in economic terms, refers to the sum knowledge of and the structure, means and methods for producing goods and services.[2] The notion of technological structure is central to economic analysis because it sets the boundaries on the amount and types of goods that can be produced, given available resources at a point in time. Technological change, on the other hand, is a dynamic process which expands these boundaries and is often said to contribute to economic growth, the latter defined as the steady process of increasing the productive capacity of the economy.[3]

Until recently, technology was regarded by many economists as exogenous to the economic system. Although technology was thought to play an important role in the economic system, very little thought was given to the factors which influenced technological change. It has only been recently that economics has begun to examine the factors which contribute to the dynamic process of technological change.

Early attempts to explain technological change focused on the role of the entrepreneur. For example, Joseph Schumpeter's hypothesis[4] was that entrepre-

---

[1] Economics may be considered to be either normative or positive. The former refers to economics or economic analyses which attempt to determine how things should be from an economic perspective, while the latter refers to analyses which attempt to determine how things will be from an economic perspective. In general this paper deals with positive economics.

[2] Graham Bannock, R.E. Baxter and Ray Rees, *The Penguin Dictionary of Economics*, (London, GB: Penguin Books, 1978).

[3] *Ibid.*

[4] Joseph A. Schumpeter, J.A., *The Theory of Economic Development*, (Cambridge, Mass.: Harvard University Press, 1934).

neurs, motivated by the expectation of monopolistic control of a market and the potential for "windfall" profits, strive to overcome established physical (technological frontier) and economic (costs) barriers in order to be the first to introduce new products in the marketplace. Today, technological change is largely determined by the research and development investment decisions of business and industry, and governments. Although, such investments in research and development (R&D) are still attempts by firms to internalize and control the potential benefits of technological change, increasingly these investments are attempts to reduce the economic uncertainty they face vis-à-vis future technological innovations.[1] Consequently, business and industry, in an effort to maintain established market shares and flexibility toward future technological trends, are at the forefront of scientific research and in so doing can influence the direction of technological change.

While it is recognized that business and industry, and governments influence technological change, it is of interest to understand what influences the directions of technological change. The hypothesis of induced innovation[2] stems from the argument that technologies will be developed to improve the productivity of the most limiting resource. The most limiting resource is either that which is the most scarce or most costly to use. The agricultural development of America and Japan demonstrated this hypothesis. For instance, in America land was abundant although labour was in short supply, while in Japan the reverse situation existed. The technologies which were developed in the two countries contributed to making their respective scarce resource more productive. Therefore, in America technologies tended to make labour more productive through mechanization, while in Japan technologies tended to make land more productive through genetic improvements, high input and intensive use of land. Given that business and industry have a choice of research activities which can influence the use of factors of production (i.e. land, labour, capital), it has been argued that it will choose the research projects which contribute the most to reducing costs. These choices, however, will be tempered by the cost of the research project itself and the existing scientific and technological frontiers that exist. Thus, inducement depends on the benefits of the innovation, the cost of the innovation and the limits of the technical frontier.

All these hypotheses are consistent with the generally accepted assumption that business decisions are made with the objective of maximizing profits and/or minimizing costs. This "bottom line" approach to technological change rarely has an ethical dimension. This is not to say that developers and adopters of technology are unethical. Rather it is a reflection of the fact that ethical factors rarely have a market cost or return, and are therefore not adequately reflected in many business decisions. Ethical problems do arise, however, when technological decisions have

---

[1]

Rob Coombs, Paolo Saviotti and Vivien Walsh, *Economics and Technological Change*, (New Jersey: Rowman and Littlefield Publishers, 1987).

[2]

Y. Hayami and V.W. Ruttan, "Factor Prices and Technical Change in Agricultural Development: the United States and Japan, 1880–1960," *Journal of Political Economy*, Vol. 78, (1970), p.1115–1141.

a negative impact on other individuals, society or the environment. Economic analysis can play an important role in assessing the consequences of such business decisions since economic analysis can include the indirect non-market costs associated with technological change to provide a truer picture of their benefits and costs to society. It can also assess the impact that alternative interventions might have in attempting to alter such business decisions to more clearly reflect the values of the society which they serve.

The Role of Government Intervention

When the aforementioned ethical problems occur, governments are called upon to intervene in an attempt to insure that the production or consumption of certain goods and services are not harmful to the well-being of society. Government intervention is often in the form of taxes or regulations which penalize or restrict the production or consumption of goods and services considered to be harmful; or in the form of subsidies which promote the production or consumption of goods and services which are considered beneficial to society. The cause of these ethical problems can be attributed to what economists refer to as "market imperfections."

In broad terms, market imperfections occur when the market does not reflect true costs or benefits to producers or consumers. An example of a market imperfection, and corresponding government interventions, is the pricing of petroleum products. From the economist's paradigm of supply and demand, the price of petroleum products is realistic—that is producers are willing to provide sufficient quantities at a price which is agreeable to consumers. The market is imperfect, however, because the price of petroleum products does not reflect the indirect societal costs of its use, such as the pollution resulting from the combustion of petroleum products.

The existence of these low cost petroleum products encouraged societies to develop and use fuel-intensive technologies. These low costs, however, did not reflect the now perceived long-term harmful effects of the adoption of such technologies. Thus the harmful effects of the adoption of such technology were not immediately translated into changes in consumption patterns, or in the development and adoption of alternative technologies. As society and governments became aware of these indirect costs, governments began to intervene with regulations, such as fuel efficiency standards, maximum emission standards; and taxes on petroleum products—all designed to reduce the consumption of petroleum products and to promote the use of alternative technologies. Some people would argue that the price of petroleum products still does not reflect the indirect costs of its use. However, not until such sentiment is translated into government policy, or the resource becomes exhausted, will the price of petroleum products rise accordingly and encourage the use of alternative energy sources.

Market imperfections also occur when the market does not adequately reflect (or price) the benefits of particular technological advances making it unprofitable for individual firms to embark on such research investments or to adopt particular technologies. Thus, government sponsorship of technologies is found in areas where the initial costs of innovation are too high for an individual or private firm to absorb but whose benefits to society would be enormous. Such technologies can be found in medical, environmental, and agricultural research. In the area of agricultural research, the development of minimum tillage practices can, in the long-run, reduce soil degradation but such technologies exhibit little immediate economic benefit to agricultural producers and consequentially to the developers of such technologies. Thus government sponsorship is necessary to promote those technologies that are highly valued by society but are often unprofitable for individual firms to develop or adopt.

The preceding examples indicate why governments choose to alter the economic factors which influence the development and adoption of technologies. However, government decisions to intervene are also influenced and curtailed by many factors which may result in counter-productive outcomes. For instance, a government with limited resources, or limited research and development capacities might decide to utilize technologies which were developed in other countries or regions. This is a position that is often taken by developing countries. Unfortunately, technologies available from developed countries reflect the "economic signals" of the developed country, and may be inappropriate for developing countries which have different levels of economic development or resource conditions. However, many governments must contend with the possibility that technologies benefit some individuals, but impose costs, or potential costs, to other individuals. In such circumstances, it must make a trade-off between social benefits and costs and private benefits or costs. For example, the government of a developing country may have to determine if the benefits derived from the promotion of a new capital-intensive technology which enhances the nation's export earnings or industrial capacity is worth more than the costs associated with the unemployment which may be caused by its adoption.

The adoption of most technologies entails accepting a certain amount of risk.[1] A factor affecting acceptable risk levels is the need to create and maintain employment. In communities with limited employment opportunities, threats of unemployment often outweigh potential health risks faced by working in unsafe work environments. These workers often oppose safety improvements if these improvements threaten the viability of the firms which employ them. Education and the media play a particularly important role in influencing the public's tolerance or intolerance of particular risks resulting from technological advances. However, the assessment of and response to these public attitudes is primarily the role of governments.

Conclusion

As noted, the market is not always capable of making the best choices in the allocation of resources. Therefore, governments or the state become charged with the responsibility to provide those goods which the market cannot supply and to adjust the price of those goods which could cause harmful side effects to society. In carrying out this task, governments attempt to influence individuals and firms to make decisions and take actions which are socially acceptable. Taxes can be used as disincentives that deter the consumption or use of particular technologies which are considered to be harmful. Subsidizes, on the other hand, can be used to

---

[1] Risk is usually measured in terms of the possible damage caused if a particular event occurred, and this multiplied by the probability of that event occurring.

encourage the consumption or development of technologies which are considered beneficial to society.

The ethical dilemma of technological change is that government intervention is not free from its own imperfections. Public policy, which has to balance social and private costs, is itself influenced by power structures or groups whose own self interest may prevent socially optimal decisions from being made as they have vested interests in maintaining the status quo. Thus private benefits are often given greater importance than societal costs. The ethical dilemma, therefore, is that the state, or more specifically the regulatory body which is to guard the interests of the general public in times of market failure, is often more concerned with protecting its own interests and perpetuating itself.

The failure of the economic system to guide us in an ethical choice of technologies is really a failure of society, or rather of the political system, to place a price on the indirect effects of technology. Society, through its mechanism of governance, could determine for instance that the users of technology or the consumers of the products of technology are to pay for the negative effects of its application. In other words, governments could introduce mechanisms to reduce pollution. But to date, few governments have been prepared to introduce norms which reflect the true value of environmental degradation or pose a serious deterrent against pollutants.

Consequently, if governments adopted a holistic approach to technology and technological development, then the economic signals could be put in place to direct our choice of technology in a manner which could be considered ethically acceptable. The economic system provides the signals which determine what technologies are developed and adopted—it does not define the moral parameters of the political system. It is society which must insure that the economic signals include their indirect costs or benefits.

DAPHNE S. TAYLOR is an agricultural economist and research assistant for the Center for Food Security, University of Guelph.
DR. TRUMAN P. PHILLIPS is Professor of Agricultural Economics, Department of Agricultural Economics and Business, University of Guelph.

11   *Frederick T. Evers*

Technology and Business Organizations: A Stakeholder Approach

> So always treat others as you would like them to treat you;
> that is the meaning of the Law and the Prophets.
> *Matthew* 7.12[1]

The "golden rule implies a reciprocal arrangement. It implies that we have agreement on what is the "proper" way to treat each other. That is, we understand an ethical or moral code and live within the code. If we expect to be dealt with ruthlessly for a particular course of action then we will respond ruthlessly when others follow that course of action. "Don't take this personally—it's just business," implies that some actions that are acceptable in a business situation would not be acceptable outside of business. This suggests that there exists a special ethical code for business dealings. The dictionary definition of ethical is "conforming to the standards of conduct of a given profession or group;" while moral means "relating to, dealing with, or capable of making the distinction between, right and wrong in conduct."[2] Thus ethical behaviour may not be "right," it is simply agreed upon as acceptable within a profession. Professions go to great lengths to define ethical codes and revise the codes over time to meet evolving standards.

The problem with business ethics is that the bounds of acceptable behaviour are not at all clear today. Milton Friedman has argued that "there is one and only one social responsibility of business—to use its resources to engage in activities designed to increase its profits so long as it stays within the rules of the game, which is to say, engages in open and free competition without deception or fraud."[3] Professor Alex Michalos rebukes this stance and in a very elegant article contends that "businesspeople ought to be morally responsible agents not merely in their roles as citizens of a moral community, but in their role as people engaged in competitive enterprise."[4]

---

[1]

The Jerusalem Bible, (Garden City, New York: Doubleday, 1966).

[2]

Webster's New World Dictionary, (New York: Simon and Schuster, 1980).

[3]

This quote from *Capitalism and Freedom* was used as the ending of an article by Milton Friedman in *The New York Times Magazine*, (September 13, 1970). The *Times* article is reprinted in *Business Ethics in Canada*, edited by Deborah C. Poff and Wilfrid J. Waluchow, (Scarborough: Prentice-Hall, 1987).

[4]

Alex Michalos, "Moral Responsibility in Business: or Fourteen Unsuccessful Ways to Pass the Buck," *Business Ethics in Canada. ibid.* pp.12–25

My premise is that even if we concede that there should be a special set of "business ethics," the milieu of business today is so complex that businesspeople find it extremely difficult to identify and play by the "rules." What is needed is a new way of thinking about ethical behaviour. Without a solution to what has become a complex reality we risk increasingly unethical responses. This was dramatized in the movie *Wall Street*, the anti-hero advocates behaviour exceeding what even the most ruthless of his colleagues would regard as acceptable. The complexity of multi-national business organizations, the global economy, and the decreasing supply of resources makes living by the golden rule very difficult. Relationships with suppliers, competitors, government agencies, special interest groups, the media, and the public contradict one another. A business simply cannot satisfy all (or even most of) those with an interest. I suggest that the stakeholder approach which has been applied to strategic planning holds great merit for this issue as well. A stakeholder is "any group or individual who can affect or is affected by the achievement of the organization's objectives."[1] The term is an expansion of "stockholder," meant to convey the reality that organizations are accountable to a larger base of individuals, groups, and other organizations than just the corporate owners. Before getting any further into the stakeholder approach, definitions of technology and business organizations and a brief discussion of the impact of technology on business organizations are needed.

Technology

The changes that are taking place in organizational complexity and the interrelationships of organizations are driven in part by technology. Technology both in a general sense and in the specific instances of innovations that are being created. Technology is hardware and software, the mechanisms used by society to convert raw materials into products and services. Technology when left unchecked grows to meet demand. Businesses create technology because there is a real (or perceived) demand for it. Technology developed within an acceptable climate causes changes in the structure of organizations and the way people think. Facsimile machines are a case in point. They combine computer and communication technology into a product that enables us to transmit documents anywhere in the world in seconds. With access to a fax machine it is possible to work up to the last minutes before a deadline and still get the results to a client on time. Hence work style has been changed—it is no longer necessary to budget for mailing or even courier time. Fax machines have not only been granted legitimacy but have also gained an intrinsic power. What business can "afford" not to have a fax machine?

Let's turn to a real life (and death) example of the interrelation of technology, business, and ethics. In the fall of 1959 Chevrolet launched the Corvair, a rear engine, air cooled automobile that was the first of its type produced in the US. According to John Z. De Lorean, at that time an executive at Pontiac, management at General Motors knew that the car was unsafe and yet went ahead with production. Many people were killed in the original Corvairs, including the son

---

R. Edward Freeman, *Strategic Management: A Stakeholder Approach*, (Boston: Pitman, 1984), p.46.

of the general manager of the Cadillac division and Ernie Kovacs, an innovative comedian in the 50s.

> There wasn't a man in top GM management who had anything to do with the Corvair who would purposely build a car that he knew would hurt or kill people. But, as part of a management team pushing for increased sales and profits, each gave his individual approval in a group to decisions which produced the car in the face of serious doubts that were raised about safety, and then later sought to squelch information which might prove the car's deficiencies.[1]

Profit was the main force in GM's decision to go ahead with the Corvairs but the fact that the technology was present to produce the car and that technologically the Corvair was new, also contributed to the breakdown of ethics.

The Corvair incident, as bad as it was, seems almost innocent compared to recent disasters. Today, the potential for disasters is even greater and disasters themselves are worse due to the complexities of technology, business and commerce. Three Mile Island, Bhopal, Chernoybl, and the Exxon Valdez conjure up images of the precarious nature of our existence with advanced technologies.

Business organizations

Organizations are pervasive in the developed world. We are born, educated, entertained, and employed in organizations. Some of us are married and some divorced in organizations. We are even buried by organizations (figuratively and literally). To understand the impact of technology on society and the relation of ethics to business we must understand organizations. Organizations can be defined as social systems, formally organized, to pursue specific goals. Useful to our analysis is to contrast the major types of organizations. Various organizational classification systems have been devised based on different dimensions. A typology (classification system using two dimensions) developed by Alfred Kuhn is based on who bears the costs and who gains the benefits of the organization.[2] Kuhn crosses costs with benefits and differentiates recipients versus sponsors. There are then four types:

(1) *cooperatives*—recipients bear the costs and gain the benefits;

(2) *profit*—recipients bear the costs while the sponsors gain the benefits;

(3) *service*—sponsors bear the costs while recipients gain the benefits; and

(4) *pressure*—sponsors bear the costs and gain the benefits.

Although all organizations must function within an ethical framework, this chapter is limited to profit type organizations, i.e., businesses. Since the recipients of businesses bear the costs then they have a "stake" in the organizations' success.

---

[1] J. Patrick Wright, *On A Clear Day You Can See General Motors: John Z. De Lorean's Look Inside the Automotive Giant*, (New York: Avon Books, 1979), pp.67–68.

[2] The typology was originally presented by Alfred Kuhn in *The Study of Society: A Unified Approach*, (Homewood, Illinois: Dorsey Press, 1963). See also Alfred Kuhn and Robert D. Beam, *The Logic of Organization: A System-Based Social Science Framework for Organization Theory*, (San Francisco: Jossey-Bass, 1982).

Hence "the customer is always right" works quite well in retail businesses. But what happens when there are many recipients and their claims on the organization differ to the extent that trying to maximize one's claim means that another's cannot be met? Clearly, what businesses do is to rank the recipients and then attempt to maximize the output to those ranked at the top. Recipients worried about health standards and environmental protection would probably argue that their concerns are ranked very low, so they try to move their priorities nearer to the top of the list. The process of identifying and trying to satisfy various recipients lends itself to a "stakeholder approach" to strategic planning.

Businesses do not like uncertainty. Businesses, like most people, want things to run smoothly—"business as usual." Due to technology, lowering of trade barriers, and increasingly scarce resources (including the labour force) businesses are now faced with constant change. The only certainty is that things will change. Business organizations use both passive and active control to lower uncertainty.[1] Passive control includes techniques such as buffering, leveling, and forecasting. Buffering is a matter of trying to protect the organization from market fluctuations. Stockpiling of raw materials in situations where the flow of the materials may be interrupted is an example of buffering. Another example is training personnel to fill positions not yet vacant. Leveling is another attempt to smooth fluctuations, e.g., airlines giving lower prices in the "off-season" to balance the number of passengers. Forecasting is carried out to predict changes that will affect the internal processes of the organization. Active control, on the other hand, involves actions that try to minimize uncertainty. Examples of active control are mergers (friendly and unfriendly) and the use of lobbying groups to promote legislative action of a particular sort. Active and passive techniques to lower uncertainty are primarily concerned with the "boundaries" of the organization. That is, these mechanisms are oriented to protecting the internal processes of the organization by managing the input of resources and the output of products and services. They are a way of taking into account suppliers, regulatory agencies, employees, and customers.

Stakeholder Approach

Managers of organizations must understand the implications of the available resources (inputs) and what they produce (outputs) as clearly as they understand the internal processes (throughputs). Traditionally, organizations were treated as closed systems both by managers and organizational scientists. More recently, structural contingency theories have emerged which treat organizations as open systems dependent upon other organizations and their milieu. Organizational processes are thought to be "contingent" upon the availability of resources (including labour), the current technology, and the presence of a market. Within

---

[1] James D. Thompson, *Organizations in Action*, (New York: McGraw-Hill, 1967), chapter 2. Passive and active control is summarized very well by Curt Tausky in *Work Organizations: Major Theoretical Perspectives*, Second Edition, (Itasca, Illinois: F.E. Peacock, 1978) pp.64–66.

the structural contingency framework universally "correct" responses to problems are not prescribed; rather decisions are based on the context of the situation. The stakeholder framework takes this one step further by proposing a systematic way of identifying all of the stakeholders. Earlier I gave Freeman's definition of stakeholder; Mitroff refines the concept further:

> Stakeholders are all those interest groups, parties, actors, claimants, and institutions—both internal and external to the corporation—that exert a hold on it. That is, stakeholders are all those parties who either affect or who are affected by a corporation's actions, behaviour, and policies.[1]

Aubrey L. Mendelow presents a stakeholder analysis for strategic planning that could be used in conjunction with a desire to achieve an ethical response to a business organization's adaptation to technological change.[2] His analysis involves identifying stakeholders, defining their attributes, and then implementing a strategic planning process that takes the stakeholders into account. The identification of stakeholders is done at both generic and specific levels. Initiating the process by listing all of the generic categories ensures that all specific stakeholders are taken into account. Stakeholder attributes that are important to consider, according to Mendelow, are orientation (for or against the organization), opinion (which can alter depending on different issues), and power (ability to affect behaviour).

We are all stakeholders in many business organizations. If the neighborhood milk store closes down because of poor sales, inability to find staff, or poor management, the neighborhood suffers. Each shopper had a stake in the store's survival. The owner no doubt opened the store to make a profit, not as a service to the neighborhood. But the store soon became a service—elderly people could walk over and pick up their groceries rather than travelling by bus and some children had their first encounters with business.

Organizational Outcomes

Organizations have outcomes—both positive and negative—for individuals, other organizations, communities, societies, and the world.[3] Positive outcomes are easy to think of: employment, products, and services. Unfortunately, negative outcomes also readily come to mind: discrimination, pollution, harmful products, inadequate services. Why are most secretaries women and most managers men? The positive outcomes make business organizations a necessary and "good" thing

---

[1] Ian I. Mitroff, *Stakeholders of the Organizational Mind: Toward a New View of Organizational Policy Making*, (San Francisco: Jossey-Bass, 1983).

[2] Aubrey L. Mendelow, "Stakeholder Analysis for Strategic Planning and Implementation," chapter 12 in *Strategic Planning and Management Handbook*, edited by William R. King and David I. Cleland, (New York: Van Nostrand Reinhold, 1987).

[3] Richard H. Hall, *Organizations: Structures, Processes and Outcomes*, Fourth Edition, (Englewood Cliffs, New Jersey: Prentice-Hall, 1987).

for society but we must also be aware of the negative outcomes and exercise our rights as stakeholders to minimize them.

The relation of ethics and technology is the most obvious with respect to negative outcomes. Some negative outcomes are intentional: dumping toxic waste into a river, selling a product known to be hazardous, or fabricating research results of clinical trials on a new drug to obtain approval from the Food and Drug Administration. Laws deter most of these practices but white collar crime is hard to detect and even harder to prosecute. Other outcomes have been called "normal accidents," inevitable occurrences due to the complexity of today's organizations.[1] Exxon did not intentionally spill over 10 million gallons of oil into Prince William Sound last March, nor did Union Carbide intentionally poison thousands of people in Bhopal, nor did NASA intentionally blow up the Challenger. These disasters were all avoidable when looked at in retrospect but instances such as these may well be inevitable given our level of technological complexity.

Another class of negative outcomes has been labelled "corporate tragedies."[2] These are instances beyond the control of the organization, e.g., the lacing of Tylenol capsules with cyanide. Distinguishing intentional from unintentional negative outcomes helps us to understand an organization's response to the outcome. Exxon is being criticized more for its slow response to the Big Spill than for the spill itself. Public perception is that the company has done little to solve the problem and has shown little regret over the incident yet, clearly Exxon is responsible for this disaster. Here we have a perfect example of the intersection of business, technology, and ethics. The technology to move millions of gallons of oil by sea exists. Businesses use this technology to make excellent profits. Along with the technology and the opportunity to make a profit must come responsibilities to all stakeholders who share in the process. This includes not just the stockholders of Exxon, but their managers, distributors, gas station operators, and customers. Exxon must look at the way it moves oil and decide if the current method optimizes the needs of all of the stakeholders in the process. In a complex society the interplay of organizations and consequences are seldom understood. Unfortunately, it takes an incident such as the Big Spill to make us conscious of how highly interconnected we all are. We tend to be reactive rather than proactive—we install a crossing guard after a child is killed at the intersection.

Conclusion

The objective of this chapter has not been to try to resolve whether business should operate on the basis of the same ethics as we would expect in other walks of life, but rather to suggest that even if we subscribe to a specialized set of "business ethics" we must rethink how to achieve these ethics. Many benefits have accrued from technology, especially when technology is viewed in a general sense; for organizations, technology can be equated to the mechanisms that enable the

---

[1]

Charles Perrow, *Normal Accidents: Living with High Risk Technologies*, (New York: Basic Books, 1984).

[2]

Ian I. Mitroff and Ralph H. Kilmann, *Corporate Tragedies: Product Tampering, Sabotage, and other Catastrophes*, (New York: Praeger, 1984).

transformation of raw materials into products. But technology has caused many changes in organizational structure, the economies of the developed nations, and in the lives of individuals. The changes are often major ones and must be reacted to quickly. The easiest solution may not always be the best. It is usually easier to buy technology than to consider its ramifications or to take people's feelings about the technology into account. Some businesspeople seem surprised when workers object to the introduction of new technologies—and yet it is a natural reaction to worry about whether one's job is about to become obsolete.

Business ethics have always been important but the complexities of technologies, global competition, and scarce resources makes them more critical and more difficult to achieve than ever before. The stakeholder approach as a technique that each organization can use to analyze its situation holds some promise. In the conclusion to her new book on management *When Giants Learn To Dance,* Rosabeth Moss Kanter offers "seven skills and sensibilities that must be cultivated if managers are to become true business athletes."[1] The third of the seven skills is to "operate with the highest ethical standards." Kanter argues that stakeholder alliances involve an element of trust; that trust is built on the mutual understanding that both parties will deal ethically. What is needed is a renewed sense of trust based on consistently ethical behaviour that sincerely tries to optimize the good of all stakeholders.

DR. F.T. EVERS is Professor of Sociology and Anthropology at the University of Guelph.

Rosabeth Moss Kanter, *When Giants Learn To Dance: Mastering the Challenges of Strategy, Management, and Careers in the 1990s,* (New York: Simon and Schuster, 1989), pp.361–365.

12　　　　　　　　　　　*Elaine Bernard*

Technology and Labour

Many in the labour movement believe we are at a crossroads with technological change. They see that new technology holds out marvelous potential for benefiting workers and all of society. At the same time, people in the workplace have experienced many problems with the introduction and application of new technology. Let me briefly review some of the positive and negative features and potential of technological change from a labour perspective.

On the positive side, there is the potential to eliminate dangerous work through either the complete automation of dangerous jobs or the close monitoring of work and conditions in potentially dangerous environments. Information technology offers the hope of eliminating tedious, repetitive, mindless work, and opens the door to limitless access to information. In many instances, we are seeing the creation of new jobs and new products. Some workers can see their skills increasing as they learn to use and modify new systems. As more information is captured electronically, the ease and speed of transmission of this information over telecommunications networks makes it possible to transfer information and work around the globe. No longer will workers in a myriad of information processing occupations have to travel to an employer's office, but they can telecommute, access their work remotely from the location of their choice, even from their homes if they like. For the most part, computer-based systems are cheaper, more energy efficient, and conservative of materials than previous technologies. These savings can be multiplied when combined with the work reorganization to eliminate wasteful duplications of records and information. In the manufacturing and industrial production area, flexible manufacturing systems can reduce the down time of machinery while increasing the flexibility in production.

On the negative side, the foremost concern is rising unemployment and the overall employment shift. The jobs that are currently being eliminated are often well paid, semi-skilled, production jobs. Much of the new employment is in the unorganized, poorly paid, service sector. There is an overall increase in part-time work, often at the expense of full-time jobs, and we are seeing the introduction of shift work into offices and clerical work. In spite of much of the positive potential of technology to eliminate tiring, repetitive jobs, new technologies have contributed in a number of areas to the "deskilling" of workers through the isolation of workers, and loss of job satisfaction through the increased use of machine-governed pacing of work. As more and more work becomes machine regulated, people become alienated from their jobs, co-workers and clients/customers. Telecommuting and work at home have seen the reintroduction of "cottage industry," only this time in information processing, and it is feared that this will undermine much of the social character of work. The ease with which computers can monitor work, down to the individual key stroke, and fraction of a second, has led to grave concerns over the invasion of privacy and continuous monitoring of workers. As well, there are a number of occupational health and safety concerns related to stress from machine regulated work, monitoring, and the extensive use of new chemicals in industrial (as well as white collar) worksites. Finally, for organized labour, there is the problem that as work moves away from centralized locations and large, permanent full-time workforces to temporary, limited-term contract employees, there are major problems in organizing the new workforce.

Technology Mystified

For labour, it's not a question of simply predicting the future, watching and waiting to see if the positive potential wins out over the negative. Labour believes that people make their own history and that the "best way to predict the future is to create it." But there are a number of significant barriers to a positive approach to the design, implementation and use of new technologies.

One of the major problems in trying to understand technological change is that technology is one of the most mystified topics in our society. It ranks second only to the economy as a phenomenon which is constantly talked about in a context guaranteed to make people feel like powerless victims—victims of technological change, or victims of economic forces.

How are normally self-assured trade unionists turned into shy, passive victims by technological change? Simple. The term "technology" becomes a catch-all phrase for a variety of new equipment, organizational changes and restructuring. Technology becomes synonymous with science and progress. Who could question science? Who would want to question progress?

For all the attention given to technology, rarely is it ever defined. This is also part of the mystification process. If we don't even know specifically what we are talking about—what technology is about—then confusion is not only understandable, it is inevitable.

Defining Technology

To demystify technology, we must define exactly what it is. Generally, in the workplace, we tend to use "technology" simply to refer to machines. But technology is a lot more than just machines. It is the means and processes through which we as a society produce the substance of our existence. It is fundamentally a human process, with people at the centre. It includes five items: tools, materials, energy forms, techniques and organization of work.

While the above five items are all components of technology, some items are more readily identified than others. The specific itemized definition is important for more than simply academic accuracy: we are finding that when unionists try to grieve or arbitrate instances of technological change, they are finding it increasingly difficult to prove that the changes are "technological changes" unless the definition in the collective agreement or in legislation is sufficiently broad to include all aspects of technology.

Let's look at each of these five items. Tools are obviously technology, whether we are talking about the historical rise of civilization and human development through tool-making or the new tools being introduced into the modern workplace, robots and computers.

New materials, on the other hand, can be almost as significant in their social impact as new tools, but changes in materials are less often recognized as important components of technology. If we think of technology change in some of the building trades, for example, plastics replacing metal and wood has been a major component of technological change. Likewise, the changeover from metal to plastic piping has spelled a massive change in plumbing.

Identifying new energy forms is one way that we have traditionally described technological revolutions. The industrial revolution of over 150 years ago is often referred to as the "steam age." There was steam before and after the steam age, but harnessing steam as an energy form, as opposed to human or animal power, revolutionized production and led to a transformation of society. Today, of course, there is much talk about the implications of nuclear energy, but the major source of power in this new information revolution is still electricity, regardless of whether it is produced by coal, hydro, or nuclear power.

The concept of technique is a little more tricky than any of the other items described so far. By "technique" we essentially mean new or different methods of doing things. A good example is in the construction industry: concrete structures are reinforced by steel. Neither material is new, but using steel mesh and beams to reinforce steel was a change in technique which greatly increased the utility of concrete in construction.

The last component of technology, and possibly the most significant in its social implications, is the organization of work. By this we are not specifically referring to unions. Organization of work refers to how we are organized in the workplace to use tool, materials, energy forms, and techniques to produce the goods or services which we as a society need to survive. Historians often characterize periods of history by noting a particular dominant organization of work can have a profound effect on the lives of working people. For example, the fundamental difference between craft and assembly line work is not a change in tools, materials, energy forms or techniques, but a change in work organization.

Technological Determinism

Aside from the practice of mystifying technology by not defining what we are talking about, an additional form of mystification imputes technology with certain powers. This is referred to as technological determinism and is reflected in the widely held beliefs that technology is unbiased, inevitable and means progress. The first step in a strategy to "create the future" is to debunk the myths that technology is unbiased, inevitable and means progress.

To deal with the issue of "bias," we should return to our definition of technology as a human process. We tend to see technology as machines, hardware, and artifacts, and therefore have a great deal of difficulty trying to imagine inanimate objects having biases. But let's look at a very familiar example: hand tools. Hand tools in North America are designed and constructed to fit an average male right hand. Left-handed people can immediately spot one of the biases in hand tools, and in fact, there are now many tools that offer right or left grips. For women, many hand tools feel awkward, uncomfortable, and difficult to manage. It may very well be because the grips are simply too wide to permit efficient control by an average woman's size hand. This is a very simple bias. For the most part it can be simply remedied by reducing the grip size. But what is important is to see that even something as inanimate as a hand tool is full of human biases and assumptions, not simply about the use of the tool, but also about the tool user.

When we get to more complex machinery such as computers or tools that mold forms of work organization, the bias is a little more difficult to spot at first. We know that when an author writes a book, the author will have a bias, and depending on his or her view of world affairs, or unions, or the economy, the bias will show in the choice of facts, emphasis and approach, and in the final product. In a similar manner, when an engineer, designer, or technician designs a machine, his or her biases will appear in the hardware and software produced by that designer. The vast majority of people currently designing machines will never have to work on the machines they are designing. In the office equipment area, the majority of designers have never worked in offices, have very little idea about what the day-to-day job of a clerical worker entails. Furthermore, they design the equipment for the purchaser, i.e. management who will never have to use it, not for the end user, i.e. the workers. Many of the current designs of machines reflect an underlying prejudice against workers. They are designed with the assumption that workers are lazy, stupid, and incompetent. Many systems designers believe that workers will purposely destroy or undermine systems if they have too much control, and much effort in design is aimed at "worker proofing" or "idiot proofing" technology. This is hardly a design prescription for social advancement and a technology for liberating humankind.[1]

The whole direction of the introduction of computers, numerically controlled tools and robots has not been to assist workers, but rather to monitor them, to replace workers altogether, or to further reduce workers' control over their work. The world is turned on its head. Technology, which is the social creation of humankind, should be its servant. In today's world, however, technology is increasingly becoming the master. Work becomes drudgery. People, a costly, unpredictable variable, are seen as the wild card in production which must be controlled or eliminated in order to make way for more predictable operations.

The view that technology is inevitable is often conjured up to undermine attempts to slow down, or change specific designs and implementations of technology. Concerns over occupational health and safety hazards, employment security, and the environment are all swept aside by the "inevitability" of technological change. And yet, there have been many examples in this and other centuries of technology being transformed by mass resistance and public pressure. Technology, like any product of human labour, is socially negotiated and mediated. This point can be illustrated by two examples.

When the telephone companies first started to market telephone service, they promoted the new technology primarily among business and professional people. They strongly discouraged the use of telephone technology for wider social purposes, especially "idle chat" and "socializing" of women. Today of course, the

Mike Cooley, *Architect or Bee? The Human/Technology Relationship,* (London: Hogarth Press, 1987), pp.40–44.

telephone industry encourages people to "reach out and touch somebody." Chat away, for as long as you like, and with someone as far away as you can afford. Social demands and the use of technology transformed telecommunications from an exclusively business and professional tool of a small minority, to a universal, private, communications tool of the majority. Telephone as we know it today, is the product of complex social interactions and transformation.[1]

Like the telephone companies of the nineteenth century, computer manufactures of the early 1970s were slow off the mark in envisioning the mass potential of computing technology. It was not IBM nor any of the large computer firms that introduced the micro computer. IBM argued that the (inevitable?) future of computers rests with users linking up to and leasing time on a few large computers in major centers. Today, of course, micro computer market has reached a point where today's most advanced micros have buried the micro vs mini distinction and the next generation will provide stiff competition to some mainframe computers. Again, here is an example where change may have been inevitable, but certainly not the specific direction taken.

The last point, that technology is progress, is one of the hardest myths to debunk. Regardless of the number of instances where we can show machines being used to replace and monitor people and to regulate the pace, quality, and rhythm of work, the vast majority of workers still have bought into the myth that technology means progress, even if they see no visible sign of progress in their own lives or workplace.

Let me use an example from the previous century to illustrate my point about how technology is not always progress. In the early 1800s coal mine owners in England approached a scientist, Humphry Davy, to assist them in reducing methane gas explosions in mines. Davy developed the "Davy miner's safety lamp" which enclosed an open flame in fine wire mesh (thereby cooling the heat from the flame to below methane's ignition point). The company heralded the invention of the Davy safety lamp as a fine example of technological progress, and even today it is often used as an example of science and industry working together to improve life for all of us.

But from the miner's point of view, the Davy safety lamp was a disaster. The lamp led to an increase in explosions and fatalities in the mines. It made it possible for company bosses to force workers into more gas intensive environments that would have been totally inaccessible before the invention of the "safety lamp." But most important, it allowed the mining companies to forestall the real improvement in mine safety—proper ventilation. Technological progress must be measured on a human scale. The Davy safety lamp may have been profitable for the mine owners, but it certainly was not progress for the miner.[2]

Aside from the general social attitudes towards technology, presuming it to be unbiased, inevitable and bringing progress, labour has a number of specific

---

[1]

Michele Martin, "Hello Central?: Technology, Culture and Gender in the Formation of Telephone Systems," (Toronto: University of Toronto, PhD, Dissertation, 1988).

[2]

David Albury and Joseph Schwartz, *Partial Progress: The Politics of Science and Technology*, (London: Pluto Press, 1982), pp.9–24.

problems in attempting to assert some control and voice in decision-making with regards to technological change. Since the 1940s our model of collective bargaining has held that management has the right to choose the tools, materials, energy forms, techniques and organization of work, and labour will essentially bargain the price of compensation for hours worked, skills acquired and years of service. Management initiates, labour responds. Increasingly today, labour recognizes that in order to mold a technology that will meet the needs of all of us, workers must have a voice in decision-making in the workplace. If new technology is going to be designed as tools of liberation, worker participation in decision-making cannot simply be an add-on, it must be integrated throughout the design, development and implementation cycle. We can not be a society of obedient, powerless slaves at work, yet free and powerful consumers after hours.[1]

Labour Transforming Technology

While labour is beginning to recognize the need for participation and control over decision-making, this challenge comes at a time when labour is under tremendous pressure. New technology has already contributed to the disciplining of labour and the declining industrial strength of the labour movement. The industrial strength of labour is essentially the power to stop or significantly slow down the production of goods and/or services resulting in dwindling profits, forcing management to negotiate with its employees. Microelectronics technology, introduced by management to increase productivity and control labour, is a key component in the reorganization which is shaking up the workplace. Other elements include growing centralization, deskilling of labour, speedups, loss of work through automation, contracting out and self-service. All are designed to undermine labour's power in the individual workplace as well as labour's collective industrial strength.

Over the last few years, labour has started to experiment with new tactics. These tactics did not arise out of the traditional strength of the labour movement, that is, its power to stop production, to go on strike. Rather, they resulted from the fact that the unions were relatively weak, which forced them to widen their support, seek new allies, and develop new tactics and alternative visions to management imposed changes. Out of these struggles labour has gained new strength. Generally these new tactics saw unions and labour organizations, the producers of goods and services, joining in common cause with consumers and community based groups. While originally adopted in the context of a limited dispute, these struggles have been broadened to get labour more involved with the community in a wider range of social issues. There are a number of examples of these types of struggles and coalitions: 1) brewery workers joining with environmentalists in opposition to the increased production of canned beer and attempts to undermine the system of

---

Canadian Labour Congress, "Workers' Rights in the Silicon Age," (Document 19, 15th Constitutional Convention, 1984).

recycling of bottled beer, 2) telephone workers organizing with chambers of commerce and community councils in small towns in order to maintain jobs and quality service for these communities, and 3) municipal workers working with environmentalists and city councils to promote recycling and environmentally sound methods of waste management.[1]

The goals in these disputes have been for the most part, defensive. The unions with their allies, are often seeking to preserve what they have: existing levels of service, universality of service or quality of goods and services. But the logic of these initiatives is to move beyond the preservation of what is, and move into the exciting terrain of what can and should be. They are attempts to create, rather than predict the future.

The recent evolution of many struggles in the labour movement which have involved mobilizing community support, hold out the hope for a transformation of the labour movement in the face of technological change. Unions are increasingly recognizing that they must contest management's vision of the future if they are to survive. Today, a social consciousness among unions and union members is a valuable asset in winning even the immediate demands of labour. When telephone workers, for example, argue for decentralized service by the telephone company, these workers are rejecting management's rights to control the quality of life of all of us. On their own, these workers and their unions do not have the power to win over management to their alternative vision but gain influence by linking with other groups in society—the local community, environmental groups, women's groups, and other advocacy groups. In this manner, they easily constitute a majority and can turn an otherwise isolated labour conflict into an important social debate.

Technology is and will continue to transform the workplace. But here, more effectively than anywhere else, through the power of organization, workers can play a major role in determining the outcome of change. Labour knows that it is no longer adequate to simply oppose management's agenda. The onus is now on labour and other groups in society to begin to construct alternative and liberating models of work and life. It is essential for the entire community that labour—the experts in the workplace—provide an alternative vision of how society can produce goods and services, minimize waste and maximize the quality of both worklife and what is produced.

DR. E. BERNARD is Director, Labour Programs in Continuing Studies at Simon Fraser University in Burnaby, B.C.

---

[1] Elaine Bernard, "New Initiatives, New Technology, New Labour," in Chris De Bresson, Margaret Lowe Benston and Jesse Vorst, *Work and New Technologies: Other Perspectives*, (Toronto: Between the Lines, 1987), pp.40–50.

Further Reading

Jones, Barry. *Sleepers, Wake! Technology and the Future of Work* (Sussex: Wheatsheaf Books Ltd., 1982).

De Bresson, Chris. *Understanding Technological Change* (Montreal: Black Rose Books, 1987).

Gill, Colin. *Work, Unemployment and the New Technology* (Oxford: Polity Press, 1985).

De Bresson, Chris; Benston, Margaret Lowe and Vorst, Jesse. *Work and New Technologies: Other Perspectives* (Toronto: Between the Lines, 1987).

Albury, David and Schwartz, Joseph. *Partial Progress: The Politics of Science and Technology* (London: Pluto Press, 1982).

Cooley, Mike, *Architect or Bee? The Human/Technology Relationship* (London: Hogarth Press, 1987).

13   *M. Anandakrishnan*

Equity and Distribution: Social Values and Technological Options

The criteria for distributive justice should be evolved, not by the considerations of charity, but by its positive influence on improving the quality of life of the majority of the people. Those who live under conditions of abject poverty would be incapable of achieving the level and quality of production of goods and services which they could otherwise reach. Moreover, an equitable distribution of the productive gains helps to improve the purchasing power of a vastly greater number of people, thereby increasing the demand for more goods and services and thus enabling higher levels of economic activities.

In spite of widespread recognition of the moral and economic imperatives of equity and distributive justice, all available evidence shows that there are still many regions of the world where the number and proportion of the absolute poor is increasing even as nations claim to have achieved economic growth, not to speak of those nations where there has been negative growth. The causes behind this unfortunate situation are being widely discussed in terms of social conditions, economic policies and political directions.

The effects associated with population growth, urbanization, lack of basic amenities of life, rapid deterioration of resource base, the debt burden, growing threats of many kinds of global problems and so forth, have come under detailed scrutiny. The object of this scrutiny is to determine the ways to deal with these complex problems in the face of existing conditions of severe resource limitations, which is likely to continue in the foreseeable future. In this context, many hopes are raised by increasing the output per given unit of resource with the use of new technologies and new organizational methods. This paper is confined to the examination of this last aspect as relating to considerations of equity, especially in the majority of developing countries.

Production and Access

Increasing the production of goods and services is only half of the problem. The real challenge of the other half of the problem lies in enabling the poor majority to have the income to buy these goods and services or to have the means to produce or to exchange the essential items needed by them. The anomaly of growing numbers of undernourished people in the face of food surpluses in many countries of the Asian region, and in some of the major food exporting Latin American countries, is testimony to this challenge. The so-called Green Revolution simply by-passed the African region. Despite the demonstrable claims of

technological miracles in increasing the production in agriculture and industries, there are now serious questions raised as to why these anomalies persist and how can they be remedied.

Lessons from the Past

It is becoming evident that no amount of technological advances can bring about equitable distribution if there is no change in the distorted patterns of ownership of productive assets and in the power structures of decision-making. For instance:

- The successful adoption of high-yielding varieties of food production was not possible in those developing countries where the farm-land was owned by a small minority, and where the agricultural policies and

institutional infrastructures did not favour access to the technologies
and agricultural inputs to the largest number of small farmers.

- The distribution of benefits of increased farm production was more
equitable in those societies where the attention was not simply focussed
on agricultural yield alone but on developing complimentary
employment opportunities, health care benefits, education and
environmental protection.
- Development of mega-industrial complexes resulted in worsening the
problems of hyper urbanization. Societies which paid serious attention
to small and medium enterprises achieved greater productivity and
distributed growth.
- Investment in research and development of areas irrelevant or
marginally relevant to the priority problems of the society have failed
to register either public support or long-term viability.

Watching the New Technological Trends

There is no real evidence to show that the euphoria behind the new technological developments will contribute towards greater distributive justice unless there are major organizational changes based on change in social values.

The rapid advances in micro-electronics, information technologies, computers, new materials and space technologies require large capital investments in high-intensity research and development. The scale of investments needed in these technologies pre-ordain the concentration instead of distribution of power, knowledge, production and gains. No doubt, there are potentials for decentralization of production activities facilitated by the use of these technologies. But the benefits of the decentralization will still be felt by a relatively smaller section of the population in the developing countries.

On the other hand, there are new technologies, especially in the areas of biotechnologies and energy technologies, with affordable research and development intensity and with a very wide scope of application in the developing countries. Even in this case, there is no guarantee that their proliferation and use will reduce the differentials between the rich and poor without current institutional change.

For instance, the new animal reproduction techniques facilitate the production of hundreds of embryos from elite parents. These are transported across continents in small freezers for use in any location, obviating the need for expensive transport of full grown animals. Benefits of this technique to the small farmers are not likely to be automatic if there are no infrastructure to enable them to access them conveniently, whereas rich farmers will have the resources to gain quickly from the advantages.

Similarly, the present pattern of use of computers, communication technologies and information systems show that they are working decidedly in favour of those who already possess some initial advantages in the society.

The investments in primary and secondary education in many developing countries have shown a marked reduction in recent years even as there has been a major leap towards higher education. This trend is disturbing not only because of the impact on the quality of life in the short term, but also because of the implications for the distribution of income in the long term and on the propagation of democratic values.

Apparent Social Values

The technological options, therefore, are not simply matters of "sourcing," choosing and adapting technologies to increase production or to gain competitive advantages. The options must be based on priority demands of society which in turn are determined by their social values.

In many societies, traditional social values have been replaced by social values as determined by individual or organized power groups. These are mostly divorced from the deeper social aspirations of larger sections of the population. A prerequisite to enable the deeper values to resurface is by promoting the national policy dialogues among the stakeholders to all walks of society including the socially affected groups in determining the areas of priority attention. Then, and only then, will the directions for technological options emerge towards the goals of reducing the inequities.

Otherwise, the inequities of technological options will manifest themselves in industrial complexes and smokestacks rather than in upgrading traditional sectors; in large hospitals with expensive gadgets rather than in rural health clinics; in prestigious R&D laboratories rather than in technology service centres; in investments for research on cash crops rather than in food crops; in massive (and polluting) power generating systems rather than in decentralized and renewable energy facilities; and in centralized bureaucracy rather than in participatory decision-making.

M. ANANDAKRISHNAN is Deputy-Director, United Nations Centre for Science and Technology for Development (UNCSTD).

The views expressed in this chapter are those of the author and do not necessarily reflect those of the United Nations.

Further Reading:

Bhalia, Ajit S. and Dilmus, James (eds.). *New Technologies and Development Experiences in Technology Blending* (Boulder, Colo.: Lynne Rienner Publishers, 1987).

Brown, Lester. *State of the World 1989: A World Watch Institute Report on Progress Toward a Sustainable Society* (New York: W.W. Norton & Co., Inc., 1989).

Hoffman, Kurt and Howard Rush. *Micro-electronics and Clothing* (New York: Praeger, 1988).

Inter-American Development Bank. *Economic and Social Progress in Latin America* (Washington, D.C.: Inter-American Development Bank, 1988).

Johnston, Ann and Sasson, Albert (eds.). *New Technologies and Development* (Paris: UNESCO2, 1986).

Nagai, Michio (ed.). *Development in the Non-Western World* (Tokyo: The United Nations University, 1984).

Smuckler, Ralph H. with David F. Gordon. *New Challenges New Opportunities* (East Lansing, Michigan: Michigan State University, 1988).

UNICEF. *The State of the World's Children 1989* (New York: UNICEF, 1989).

UNIT V
QUALITY OF LIFE AND
SOCIAL JUSTICE

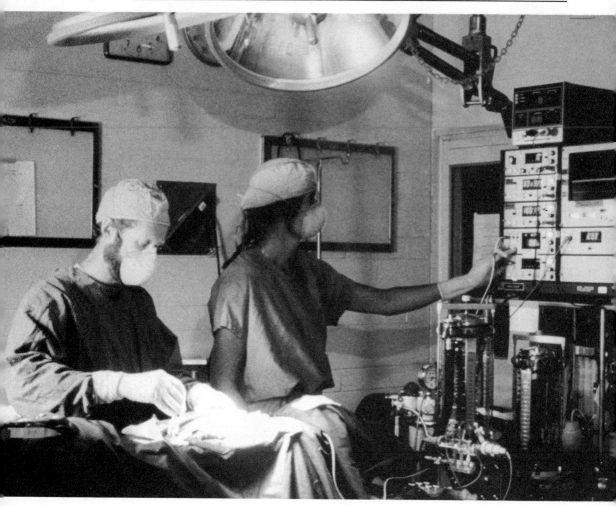

David J. Roy

The Health and Life Sciences: Where Is the Ethics for our Knowledge and Power?

Some may still share the belief of the sardonic writer of Ecclesiastes that there is nothing new under the sun, and, in this spirit, follow Nietzsche's eye as he scans the eternal return of the same. But more likely, most of us fix our gaze wonderingly or apprehensively on the new and astounding power over life amassed from cumulative progress in the life sciences. Some rejoice and others fear that nothing will ever be the same again.

We should make no mistake about it. Things are changing fast, particularly in the areas of diagnostic technology, organ replacement and life-prolongation, in reproductive biology, the neurosciences, genetics, and molecular biology. The results of research and technological development along the front of so many specializations are not only cognitive. We are acquiring the power to do things for, with, and to human beings that could never be done before. All this entails levels of ethical challenges to existing value systems. These levels could be grouped into four categories arranged along a continuum.

Levels of Ethical Challenge

I. Some of the changes that we can effect today, though technically phenomenal, are ethically prosaic. They simply buttress traditional and accepted values. Vaccines and antibiotics are an example. Of course, the testing of candidate vaccines, as in the case of HIV infection, can pose formidable challenges.

II. Other developments are ethically paradoxical. They set up difficult value conflicts. Our medical, surgical, and technical powers to prolong life have given thousands of people renewed time to realize their dreams. These same powers have spawned widespread movements mobilized by the plea for dying with dignity. Now again in the 1980s, as several times earlier in this century, voices are rising to argue that for many, active euthanasia is the only way to assure death with dignity. Short of active euthanasia, there is now widespread recognition that prolonging life at all costs, particularly at costs the patient cannot bear, is not the right thing to do. But conflicts abound each year about going too far versus not going far enough in prolonging the lives of patients in neonatal units, geriatric units, cancer clinics, in neurology units and in the care of persons with AIDS.

III. Other advances in the broad domain of biomedicine are socially and ethically dramatic. Advances in reproductive biology and technology, for instance, now offer the power to alter radically the recurrent drama of reproductive behaviour and reproductive relationships. The scientific and technical ability to harvest ova, to construct human embryos in the laboratory, to freeze, thaw or otherwise manipulate these embryos before transfer, offer alternatives to infertility that challenge our system of law and our traditional ethics of the family. If we can now cut the biological roots of the family, how can we apply the ethics of biologically rooted reproduction to these new technologies?
Innumerable working groups, commissions, and conferences over the past fifteen years have forged a consensus on the general ethical acceptability of artificial insemination (AID), in vitro fertilization (IVF), and gamete intrafallopian transfer (GIFT), as techniques of assisted reproduction. But ethical controversy is still widespread on such matters as ovum and embryo donation; multiple transfer of embryos and ova; the use of fetal reduction (selective abortion) in multiple pregnancies resulting from ovarian stimulation, as well as from the multiple transfer of embryo and ova; surrogate motherhood; the storage of frozen human embryos and the conduct of scientific research on embryos constructed in the laboratory.

IV. Some people fear that advances in molecular biology and genetics could prove to be ethically meta-dramatic, that is, could take us into realms of action that go beyond the drama or condition that we have called human for thousands of years. In the 1970s, during the debates on recombinant DNA technology, Shaw Livermore described this early advance in molecular biology as delivering a powerful means of changing the order of life.[1]

Our society harbours quite antithetical attitudes about progress in genetic science and technology. The fear of some is that science may inch forward to a nearly total understanding of the human genome and spawn the technologies to manipulate and modify uniquely human characteristics. The prospect that human nature, taken for centuries as the principle of the common good and the public purpose, could be reduced to the status of a technological project has generated anxiety and dismay.

Others, including leading thinkers who are not scientists, have emphasized that recombinant DNA technology rejuvenated molecular biology and created space for the design of industrial, pharmaceutical, and medical projects that promise great benefit to all. The nascent ability to master the genetic correlates of disease may well lead to a profound transformation of medical theory and practice, perhaps eventually to the eradication or alleviation of diseases that cause untold human suffering. What is most feared within this perspective is that the possibil-

Prof. Shaw Livermore quoted in: William Bennett and Joel Guerin, "Science that Frightens Scientists. The Great Debate over DNA," *The Atlantic Monthly*, February 1977, p.59.

ities of distant mischief could be used to block or seriously hamper highly promising initiatives in one of the most flourishing areas of contemporary science.

We cannot, of course, think clearly about the ethical future of genetics without penetratingly analyzing its past. Benno Muller-Hill has advanced the thesis that the rise of genetics is marked by a giant repression of its history,[1] that is, that history harboured a strong eugenic rejection of the principle that all human beings are created equal. As geneticists and all of us in society critically observe advances in genetic science and technology, we will have to heed Loren Graham's advice and pay close attention to the second-order links between science and values. These connections are not abstract. The second-order links depend on existing political and social situations, on current and future technological power, and on the attraction of currently dominant beliefs and ideologies. The latter are particularly crucial from an ethical viewpoint, and all the more so when they are simultaneously flawed, persuasively argued, and dazzlingly articulated.[2]

The Control of Science?

How the scientific community should relate to the broader human community in free societies is an enduring question, one rejuvenated with each new generation and each major scientific innovation. There have been frequent occasions over the past fifteen years to subject this issue to penetrating scrutiny in the biomedical sciences. The relationship has become a problem and remains an issue since the answers to the questions about how the directions of scientific advance should be determined, and about how scientific research should be monitored, are still sources of controversy.

The very possibility of public participation in shaping the future course of scientific advance, and of any related outgrowth of technological innovation, depends upon the fulfillment of at least three conditions:

1. Public acquisition and comprehension of precise information about discoveries in a range of related basic sciences. This is essential since a future direction of scientific and technological innovation is a cumulative resultant from several or many lines research.
2. Public access to reasonable extrapolations or scenarios that connect these discoveries to the common good and public purpose.
3. Procedures that can reliably evaluate the future impact on the common good and public purpose of scientific and technological development, likely to result from basic discoveries.

It is unlikely that these three conditions can regularly be fulfilled, if ever at all, in time to assure public participation in determining the "rules of the game." Although it may be too late for a public awakening to the quiet beginnings of a scientific revolution, even a late public awakening is salutary. The question,

---

[1]

B. Muller-Hill, "Genetics After Auschwitz," *Holocaust and Genocide Studies*, Vol. 2, No. 3 (1987), p.20.

[2]

L.R. Graham, "Political Ideology and Genetic Theory: Russia and Germany in the 1920s," *Hastings Centre Report*, (1987), Vol. 7, pp.30–39.

however, is whether genuine, and potentially very beneficial, scientific development would not be seriously disturbed and derailed by the premature meddling of persons and groups unequipped to conceive, let alone evaluate, future impacts that can, at any early period of science, be only dimly intimated, even by the most trained and perspicacious of minds?

Ethics in Crisis?

The foundations of contemporary ethics have crumbled. We repeatedly find it difficult, at times impossible, to distinguish right from wrong and, indeed, on matters that we know are critical for the fate of individuals and communities. We have either lost the reference system that would permit us to decide with solidarity and moral assurance which value may, or has to be sacrificed, or we have created a world that continually engenders tragedies, situations in which people of good will are forced to practice moral triage.

Ethics is in a foundational crisis because earlier intelligible orders that exercised sway over the mind and created a community of moral meaning have disintegrated or are in the process of doing so. A new intelligible order, a new unified moral field theory has not yet arrived. A new and vigorous voluntarism is arising within the space created by the disappearance of morally normative intelligible orders. Choice is the norm and choice becomes "an act of will responsible to nothing beyond itself."[1] If the moral boundaries of an intelligible order for human living no longer hold, there is no conceivable constraint on what we shall try, no imaginable perimeter at which we shall stop, for human desire per se has no internal limits. Today's crisis, as Hans Jonas would propose, emerges from the combination of an "anarchy of human choosing with the apocalyptic power of contemporary man—the combination of near-omnipotence with near-emptiness."[2]

The task of ethics is to illuminate the conditions for consistency between knowing and doing. However both theory and practice are in a constant state of flux. Is it at all possible to discover a solid foundation for ethics in a cultural period marked by radical innovation and the impermanence of yesterday's ideas? Of course, science is human knowledge and the power of technology lies in the hands of human beings and within the scope of human design. Perhaps, the principle and the foundation of ethics is to be found within human nature. That may be true. But the method of the past leaves room for doubt. Traditional moral norms were grounded in the uniqueness, some would hold, in the sacredness of human life. Can we now ground ethics in the experience of sacredness when modern science and technology exhibit evidence in favour of reductionism and a diminishment of

---

[1]
Brand Blanshard, *Reason and Goodness*, (New York: Humanities Press, 1967), p.254.
[2]
H. Jonas, *Philosophical Essays*, (Engelwood Cliffs: Prentice-Hall Inc., 1974), p.176.

the high status accorded to human life in cultures that appear mythic within the horizon of modern science?

Recent experiments utilizing gene transfer from one species to another show that genes are interchangeable. The idea that the genetic components of human life are, at an elementary level, interchangeable with those of all other life has led one scientist to wonder "if there is anything unique about humanness."[1] How can a normative ethics of sufficient stature to match the power of novel technologies be constructed on the shifting sands of an "image of man" that commands no reverence?

Toward a Global Ethics?

Human action, potentiated by modern science and technology, now exercises effects that encompass the planet, all levels of the biosphere, and reach far into the future. How can a microethics, based on the neighborhood and village relationships of immediacy, illuminate the demands of responsibility for actions that are global, that determine the fate of future generations, and that can modify structures and institutions long thought to be solid and unchangeable components of nature and human nature?

Every major domain of human activity today affects the lives of nearly everyone on this planet and will set up chains of consequences that will profoundly predetermine the mode and even the possibility of life of future generations. The effects of nuclear energy and nuclear armaments, of multinational corporate economics, of satellite-mediated global communications, and of powerful new biotechnologies—to mention only a few examples—transcend the microsphere (the family, neighborhood, city) and the mesosphere (the level of the nation) to impact upon the macrosphere (the level of the planetary community). We now need a global ethics as we never have before.

Achieving a macroethics of planetary scope demands a radical transformation of our sense of community, our attitudes of allegiance, our dominant value systems, our related norms and criteria of decision, choice and action. Traditional ethics have been patterned on the microsphere. We have not yet reached an ethics to govern and guide the activities of nations. National interest is the ultimate norm and Machiavellian power politics still dispenses with the need for moral justification of national policies. How can we ever attain a sense of community, a system of values, and a normative ethics of transcultural and transnational scope?

Ethics in Open Societies

The *Canadian Charter of Rights and Freedoms* stipulates that the rights and freedoms it guarantees are subject only to limits that are reasonable, legally prescribed, and demonstrably justified in a free and democratic society.[2]

---

[1] Constance Holden, "Ethics Panel Looks at Human Gene Splicing," *Science*, (August 6, 1982), Vol. 217, p.517.

[2] The Canadian Charter of Rights and Freedoms, "A Guide for Canadians," (Ottawa: Ministry of Supply and Services, 1984), para. 1.

Justification by argument in a free and democratic society exerts an impact on what we hold to be reasonable, ethically acceptable, and legally tolerable. Of course, our society is highly pluralistic. We do not all share the same ethos: we differ on the level of fundamental beliefs, perceptions, and assumptions about the origin and destiny of human life, and about the scope of human rights and human dignity. We differ on the level of morality. We do not all share the same value hierarchy. We are not unanimous in our persuasions about what values may be sacrificed to protect others when all cannot be maintained or achieved simultaneously. We differ at times on what values must be protected and maintained at all costs, or nearly so.

Reasonableness, then, is not homogeneous in a free and democratic society. the Scots poet, Robert Burns, enunciated the following principle of ethics: "Whatever grips your honour, let that your border be." We differ, as individuals and as groups, about what our sense of honour demands. The law and the variant moralities in our society set borders at different levels and in very differing ways. The overarching question to all of us in societies that are both graced and challenged by high science and technology is: how can we mediate or accommodate the variant tendencies to set moral borders in very different places, and how can we do so in a way that maintains the reality, not just the guise, of a free and democratic society?

DR. D.J. ROY is Director, Center for Bioethics at the Clinical Research Institute of Montreal.

15   *Michael McDonald*

Ethics Versus Expertise: The Politics of Technology

This chapter will sketch some of the main features of the politics of technology in order to draw some lessons and raise some questions.[1] By the *politics of technology*, I mean the ways in which we as a culture and society authoritatively decide about which technologies to encourage or discourage through a whole variety of social means. These include both informal means of influence such as attitudes of approval and disapproval and the awarding of social status, and formal means of state power such as planning rules, tax structures, and legal prohibitions. The politics of technology come sharply into focus in Canada and in a number of other national and international jurisdictions, in official hearings, including those held by Royal Commissions, commissions of enquiry, regulatory and licensing bodies, legislative committees, and administrative tribunals. The hearings may focus on exotic technologies such as nuclear power and genetic engineering or more mundane technologies such as the licensing of herbicides and pesticides; siting a gravel pit, garbage dump or highway; or the preservation of an environmentally sensitive site like a swamp. In such hearings, I see a kind of ritual combat between those who present an essentially technological case and those who advance self-consciously ethical arguments. The combatants are like two opposing peoples—each with its distinct language, customs, loyalties, and sacred texts.

Insiders: These are technical experts who advance arguments based on their fields of expertise. Sometimes the expertise is quite discipline specific: landfill management, biotechnology, nuclear engineering, or one of the agricultural sciences. At other times, the experts make a cross-disciplinary claim to authority on

[1]

A major source of material of this chapter comes from my work as Principal Investigator on the report, *Towards a Canadian Research Strategy for Applied Ethics*. My co-researchers were Prof. Marie-Helene Parizeau (Laval University) and Mr. Daryl Pullman (University of Waterloo). This *Report* was prepared for the Canadian Federation for the Humanities (CFH) for submission to the Social Sciences and Humanities Research Council of Canada in November 1988. Copies of the *Report* are available from CFH at 151 Slater Street, Suite 407, Ottawa, Canada K1P 5H3.

My work in this chapter also owes a great deal to the current research of my colleagues, Professors Lawrence Haworth and Conrad Brunk, on risk-benefit analysis and in particular to Brunk's masterful paper, "Professionalism and Responsibility in the Technological Society" which first appeared as the 1985 Benjamin Eby Lecture in *The Conrad Grebel Review*, 3 February 1985, and is now available in *Business Ethics in Canada*, D. Poff and W. Waluchow, (eds.), (Scarborough, Ont.: Prentice-Hall Canada, 1987) pp.60–75.

the basis of knowledge of such areas as epidemiology, planning, and particularly risk-benefit analysis. The acquisition of disciplinary and cross-disciplinary expertise requires a long period of apprenticeship to learn the language and acquire technical skills. This is followed by various rites of initiation, including the bestowal of advanced degrees and professional status. These experts come from a variety of places: government ministries, regulatory bodies, corporations, consulting firms and academic institutions. Not surprisingly, most of the experts are to be found on the high side of tech outcomes in which their own institutions have a direct or indirect stake. Because experts and their expertise "do not come cheap," they are usually lined up on the side of the more powerful institutions in our society—corporations and bureaucracies. In short, I will describe experts as *insiders*, having and defending their privileged access to and use of power.

This power is dependent on the preservation of their authoritative knowledge and prestige as experts and professionals. Most often they are viewed and view themselves as *professionals* in the broad sense of the term i.e. as having on the basis of their training and experience, access to esoteric and relatively inaccessible bodies of knowledge; and sometimes, also as professionals in the narrower sense of the term, as having professional accreditation (e.g. a professional engineer, agronomist, medical doctor or lawyer). A natural corollary of the claim to professional expertise is what might be considered as an attitude favouring *professional hegemony*. This attitude rests on the belief that in the area of technical expertise, which is defined by the profession, issues are to be decided by rigourous standards of evidence and argument, which again the profession defines. Now I want to suggest that the aforementioned statement (A) is a key premise in an argument that winds up with the conclusion that the main issues in such hearings are essentially technical ones to be settled on the basis of the best technical information and, thus, on the basis of their professional expertise. This conclusion will be referred to as (Z).

Before looking at their opponents, I should make three comments about the argument from premise A to Z. First, most experts do not actually try to construct an argument for Z; rather on the basis of a commitment to a few more premises, the expert slides or leaps from A to the conclusion Z. Second, the argument is what logicians describe as an enthymeme because it is missing those additional premises (B, C, D, ..., Y) which would make it a valid argument[1]. One cannot conclusively defeat enthymatic arguments because it is not possible to exhaustively list and then counter every conceivable missing premise. While I do believe that there is no *plausible* valid argument from A to Z, my purpose here is to think through what happens when experts accept Z on the basis of A and additional (unspecified) premises. Third, I do not believe that technical experts will consciously rehearse the argument from A to Z but that they will act or respond as if they accepted such an argument at face value. In other words, especially when

---

[1]

In "Professionalism and Responsibility in the Technological Society," Brunk has done a splendid job of identifying such key missing premises as faith in Invisible Hand arguments, including the free market economic system, "the free market of ideas," and the existence of a "technological fix" for all technological problems (pp.68–69).

insider-experts are criticized by outsiders, the experts react as if professional judgement and competence is the sole issue.

Outsiders: Having described the insider experts, I will now describe the outsiders. I have in mind groups of citizens, whether organized into local, national or international groups (Pollution Probe, Friends of the Earth, the Green Movement, etc.) or loose coalitions of individuals or groups whether united in opposition, say, to situating a dump site in their backyards, or in support, say, of the preservation of an environmentally sensitive area. Like insiders, outsiders have their own language(s) and tribal loyalties. But they can be distinguished from insiders in four important respects. First of all, they are outsiders in the sense of lacing access to special or privileged levers of power. Their power, such as it is, derives from the rights that ordinary citizens have in a democratic society, including the use of the ballot box, the possibility of organizing into pressure groups, and whatever publicity our highly centralized media gives them and their cause(s). Second, their main appeal is to moral arguments, usually either non-maleficence {Do not harm} or beneficence {Do good}. Third, as ordinary citizens, they lack and cannot afford the expertise to argue on an even footing with insider experts. Fourth, even where they have access to such expertise—often from supporters in the academic community—they are reluctant to base their arguments on technical testimony; for they believe the real issues are moral and not technical.

Moreover, they may well be convinced that appeals to technical authority are essentially undemocratic—removing power from the hands of the people and putting it in the hands of experts who act on behalf of big business or big government. In short, the outsiders are by and large "moralists."

Insiders Versus Outsiders: I would now like to reflect on the clash of insiders and outsiders and, in particular, how these antagonists see each other. The clash is very often what can be described as "a non-meeting of minds"—not just in the sense that they support opposing outcomes, but more importantly and interestingly in the sense that they do not join issue with each other. The insider-experts present the view that important issues are essentially technical issues; whereas, the outsider-citizens take the position that these are moral issues. They are like the proverbial ships passing in the night. There is an interesting dynamic at work here that can only be understood if we think about (a) how each group sees the other and then (b) how as a result, each receives confirmation and reinforcement of its self-image.

Consider the clash from the insider perspective. The insiders see themselves as presenting the conclusions of their hard-won research and training efforts. By not joining issue with them on these technical grounds, outsiders behave in a way that confirms the insider's image of themselves as "reasonable" and "responsible" persons, and their image of outsiders as "irrational" (i.e. emotional) and "irresponsible." Moreover, outsiders are seen as denigrating the insiders' authority as experts either directly by questioning their sincerity and professionalism and scientific detachment or indirectly by dismissing that expertise as irrelevant or peripheral to the dispute.

In such circumstances, it is not surprising that insiders regard outsiders as presenting an argument that is (a) irrelevant and (b) requiring not so much a direct response but an effort in public relations, in particular in *damage control* in the event of a disaster like Bhopal or the oil spill at Valdez, Alaska early this year.[1] When hearings are before a tribunal that takes an essentially technical approach to its task, the first (a) is the favoured tack; this is reflected in the conduct of expert witnesses and the tribunal. When the hearings are before an essentially political body, like a legislative committee, then the second (b) is more in evidence as expert witnesses are chosen as much for their political astuteness on the stand as for their professional capabilities. Finally, all this reinforces the expert community's self-image as speaking with the calm, dispassionate and value-free voice of science and not as essentially privileged insiders.

From the outsider perspective, the experts do look like insiders—basically as gatekeepers protecting vested interests. The experts' self-image as value-free scientists is seen as an essentially amoral, if not immoral, stance. Frozen out of access to power, outsiders behave as insiders expect, namely, by increasingly resorting to political means and forums for promoting the outsider cause. And of course, the insiders do what the outsiders expect by standing on their expertise and treating any other approach as essentially one of public relations. Public apprehension of the insider-outsider dispute varies. In the absence of a crisis,

---

The oil spill at Valdez, Alaska in March 1989, the largest in North America's history, has been described by Exxon's spokesperson as "a mishap."

outsiders look like prophets of doom and insiders like the calmly competent managers of a highly acceptable status quo. In times of crisis, the image shifts radically: the public identifies with outsiders and sees insiders as manipulative and untrustworthy. So at times, the public perception is that the cloak of virtue wears thin; while at other times, it is that the umbrella of technical expertise is full of holes.

Expertise Without Ethics or Ethics Without Expertise

Both alternatives are extremely unfortunate. On the one hand, the expertise without the ethics option is short-sighted and dangerous. It also masks assumptions about knowledge and values on which the experts base their claims to the gatekeeper role in society. These assumptions include the following:

- that there is a sharp and clear separation of "scientific" and "normative" issues
- that science is "objective" and ethics is "subjective"
- that the objective should rule the subjective
- that science is worth pursuing both for its own sake and for the sake of its technological results
- that the experts can be trusted.

On the other hand, the ethics without expertise option is, as it stands, a non-starter in a world in which technology is so pervasive. Even if we wanted to wholly undo modern technology—and very few outsiders, I believe, really want that—we would have to understand what it is we were undoing. There is also here an unrealistic faith in the powers of regulation by governments. What is missed is the fact that in all societies and particularly in our kind of society, a great deal depends on *self-regulation*—the informed and voluntary internalization and acceptance of moral norms, that is, self-regulation on an individual level and, even more importantly, on a social level. In the latter regard, the self-regulation of experts and professionals is indispensable. What is really in dispute between the insiders and outsiders is not, as they both believe, whether experts shall be moralized but how they shall be moralized! In particular, the issue is whether experts owe their primary loyalties to their own institutions or whether their primary loyalties are owed to the general community and its common good.

Both the expertise without ethics and the ethics without expertise positions rest on the naive belief that the moral issues posed by modern technology are simple and clear. (Of course, outsiders and insiders take diametrically opposed positions on what it is that is simple and clear). In my research for the report *Towards a Canadian Research Strategy for Applied Ethics*, I was told by representatives of the Canadian scientific research community that ethics simply doesn't enter into the question of investment in scientific research, other than in ascertaining that the research funded is not in violation of protocols on research with human and animal subjects. There seemed to be no realization that a decision to fund research in even the most benign areas of research, such as medicine, could lead to morally unacceptable results. For instance, a serious shift in scarce medical dollars to provide transplants for a few Canadians as opposed to chronic care for many even more seriously ill Canadians. On the other side, a prominent outsider told me that in a rapidly over-populating world, it was self-evident that Canada had to radically decrease its population and standard of living. Here, serious issues of cultural continuity, moral relationships of rich to poor nations, complex interdependency, and intergenerational obligations were dismissed with a wave of the hand.

To conclude, let me offer a modest but important suggestion about one way of joining ethics and expertise. This is to promote research and teaching in the area of applied ethics. This is an area in which the whole point is to look seriously at the problems of technology, professionalization and other issues touched on in this chapter from a moral perspective. The end result of applied ethics is neither more expert opinions in arcane areas of knowledge nor moral diatribes against the forces of evil; it is rather a better understanding of the major moral issues before us. The end result is, in short, a necessary beginning.

DR. M. MCDONALD is Professor of Philosophy at the University of Waterloo.

UNIT VI
POWER, POLITICS, AND FREEDOM

16   *Martha J. Bailey*

"Lamenting Some Enforcèd Chastity": Reproductive Freedom, Law, and the State

The moon methinks looks with a wat'ry eye;
And when she weeps, weeps every little flower,
Lamenting some enforcèd chastity.

> William Shakespeare, *A Midsummer Night's Dream*,
> Act III, Scene One, Lines 198–200.

Titania's words of pity for another's "enforcèd chastity," spoken as she exists to enjoy her own sexual freedom, prefigure the initial impetus of the twentieth-century feminist claim to reproductive freedom. From the early 1960s, feminists fought to separate sex from reproduction, through contraception and abortion, in order to liberate women's sexuality. Of course, the freedom Titania exercised is illusory—Oberon, impatient with Titania's wilfulness, has "magicked" her into desiring Bottom, who has been turned into an ass for the occasion. Titania experiences her sexual intercourse with this animal as an act of free choice, then, no longer under Oberon's spell as she awakes the next day, Queen Titania shamefully remembers what she hope has been a dream. The experience has chastened her; she is now tamed, rather like Kate the shrew.

Titania's story captures the double-edged nature of reproductive freedom for women. Contraception and abortion—the right *not* to reproduce—not only liberated women's sexuality, but also made women more sexually available for men. Technological advances and decriminalization in the areas of contraception and abortion, while separating sex from reproduction—a necessary condition for gender equality—do not transform the traditional terms of heterosexual sex. Women have reexamined their experience of sexual freedom during the '60s and '70s, recognizing that the sexual ideology of the time served a male fantasy of endlessly available sex. The fact that both *Playboy* and feminists support contraception and abortion does not necessarily mean that the sexual values of *Playboy* will always prevail, but legal and technological developments cannot be assessed without an understanding of the male interests at stake, and, given current power relations, a hypothesis that those interests will be given priority.

The other side of reproductive freedom—the right to reproduce—has more recently become a focus, as the technology relating to artificial insemination by donor (AID), surrogacy (a misnomer because it wrongly suggests that the biological and gestational mother is standing in the place of the real mother), *in vitro* fertilization, and embryo transfer, has developed. Of course, surrogacy and AID are not necessarily technological, but they have developed as such in our medicalized society because of the methods employed (e.g. freezing sperm instead of using a turkey baster for AID to making screening possible). The right to reproduce, like the right not to reproduce, can be used by and against women. Reproductive technologies may benefit some women, but have the potential to reinforce class and race oppression of others—poor white women serve as surrogates; poor women of colour provide wombs for embryo transfers.

In contrast with abortion and contraception, women have not initially focused on the right to use reproductive technologies, but rather on controlling the terms on which these technologies are offered. The feminist claim to the right to reproduce has primarily centred on attacking enforced or coerced sterilization and abortion and demanding social support for parenting, rather than in claiming unregulated access to reproductive technologies. Although the right to reproduce without having sex is central to women's reproductive freedom, and has benefited some women in an important way (for example the use of AID by lesbian women), feminists, so far, have given more energy to positioning themselves against oppressive use of reproductive technologies than to developing claims for access on their own terms.

There *is* a feminist argument in favour of the right of women to exercise their autonomy by, say, entering into surrogacy contracts, and some women have argued against state interference with women's use of technology. "If you believe in pro-choice for abortion, I think one has to believe in pro-choice for embryo freezing," says Jennifer Hillman, a woman who wants to take advantage of this new technology, and who recognizes reproductive technology as the flip side of women's reproductive freedom.[1] Arguments in favour of reproductive rights, in contrast with abortion, have not as generally involved positive rights claims, that is, demands for state provision of services and universal access, although there are exceptions.

The state controls contraception, abortion, and reproductive technologies variously through criminalization, regulation, medicalization, and funding, and this control has run counter to the feminist project of separating sex from reproduction. Informing the state agenda are the twin dichotomies of liberalism's public/private distinction and the conceptual separation of foetus and mother. The nature and interplay of these two dichotomies find expression in the Supreme Court of Canada's judgement in *Morgentaler et al.* v. *R.* (1988 44 D.L.R. (4th) 385), and in the Law Reform Commission of Canada's 1989 report, *Crimes Against the Foetus* (Ottawa: Working Paper 58).

In *Morgentaler*, five of the seven justices who heard the case struck down s.251 of the *Criminal Code* on the grounds that it violated the fundamental right to "liberty and security of the person" guaranteed by s.7 of the *Canadian Charter of Rights and Freedoms*[2] in a manner that was not "in accordance with the principles of fundamental justice." Section 251 made abortion a criminal offence, while affording a defence for abortions deemed to be "therapeutic," that is, abortions

---

[1]

Quoted in Anne Mullens, "Technology allows embryos to be frozen until implanted," *The [Kingston] Whig Standard* 13 May 1989: 1–2 at 1.

[2]

Part I of the Constitution Act, 1982, being Schedule B of the *Canada Act 1982* (U.K.), 1982, c.11

which took place in accredited hospitals for the purpose of protecting the life or health of the pregnant woman, after approval by a committee composed of three physicians.

Chief Justice Dickson, with Lamer, J. concurring and Beetz, J., with Estey, J. concurring, stated that s.251 violated the fundamental right to security of the person. Madame Justice Wilson reasoned that s.251 not only deprives a pregnant woman of her right liberty, and it is the judgment of Wilson, J. which most clearly posits a public/private distinction. She writes, "...the rights guaranteed in the *Charter* erect around each individual, metaphorically speaking, an invisible fence over which the state will not be allowed to trespass. The role of the courts is to map out, piece by piece, the parameters of this fence."[1] The difficulty with resting the claim to abortion on this "invisible fence"—the negative rights to be left alone by the state, or the right to privacy—is that, on those terms, the state is under no obligation to provide access to abortion. In his reasons, Beetz, J. says: "The state can obviously not be said to have violated, for example, a pregnant woman's security of the person simply on the basis that her pregnancy in and of itself represents a danger to her life or health. There must be state intervention for "security of the person" in s.7 to be violated."[2] Because of *Morgentaler*, the state is no longer able to prevent women from obtaining abortions, but neither is it obliged to provide the service. In a number of Canadian provinces it remains difficult or even impossible to obtain an abortion or to get government health insurance coverage for the procedure.

Another problem with the "invisible fence" approach is the contingent right of the state to cross over the fence to protect the state's interests or the rights of another person. The foetus, though not a person, is considered a separate entity, in whose protection the state claims an interest. The state's interest in protecting the foetus is balanced against the woman's interest in liberty and security of the person and, according to the justices in *Morgentaler*, it would be constitutionally valid for the state to give priority to the foetus over the pregnant woman at some stage. Madame Justice Wilson writes:

In the early stages the woman's autonomy would be absolute; her decision, reached in consultation with her physician, not to carry the foetus to term would be conclusive. The state would have no business inquiring into her reasons. Her reasons for having an abortion would, however, be the proper subject of inquiry at the later stages of her pregnancy when the state's compelling interest in the protection of the foetus would justify it in prescribing conditions. The precise point in the development of the foetus at which the state's interest in its protection becomes "compelling," I leave to the informed judgement of the legislature which is in a position to receive guidance on the subject from all the relevant disciplines. It seems to me, however, that this might fall somewhere in the second trimester.[3]

---

[1]
  p.485.

[2]
  p.428.

[3]
  p.499.

Determining the point at which state interest in foetal protection becomes "compelling" is problematized by technological developments. In 1973, the U.S. Supreme Court decided in *Roe* v. *Wade*, 93 S.Ct 705, that the state's interest in the potential life of the foetus became compelling on viability because the foetus then has the capability of meaningful life outside the mother's womb. With advances in medical research, however, the foetus is now viable—capable of surviving outside the womb—at an earlier stage in the pregnancy. The question arises as to whether the state has a "floating" compelling interest which attaches on basis of current medical technology. Since women in the U.S. and, to a lesser extent, in Canada have unequal access to medical services, a second question is whether a compelling interest in foetal protection should be related to existing technology or a particular woman's access to that technology. In view of the fact that an embryo is now capable of survival outside the womb of the woman who conceived it, one may also ask whether the state has a compelling interest in all embryos for which a willing host (or freezer) can be found.

Success in establishing that the state's compelling interest in foetal protection should override a woman's right to abortion is conditional upon the conceptual separation of foetus and woman, a dichotomy aided by actual separation through technologies such as embryo transfers. Ultrasound images also serve this cause by allowing us actually to see the foetus as a separate entity and to ignore the pregnant woman. These powerful ultrasound images have been successfully used by members of the anti-choice movement to evoke support for their cause. Even when the invisible vessel containing the floating foetus is remembered, her interests and rights are not determinative, but simply to be balanced against those of the foetus. That the foetus has its own rights and interests—its own "invisible fence"—is all the more conceivable, for some, because of the ultrasound image of a separate entity. The issue of whether the foetus itself has a constitutionally protected right to life was left open by the Supreme Court of Canada in *Morgentaler*, and again on 9 March 1989, when the Court dismissed Joseph Borowski's claim that the law struck down in *Morgentaler* infringed the rights of the foetus as being moot.

As its title indicates, *Crimes Against the Foetus* focuses on the foetus as a separate, vulnerable potential victim in need of protection. The foetus is not presented as a person with constitutional rights, but as an entity—a form of life—deserving of a level of state protection somewhere between that accorded persons and that given to non-persons. The Law Reform Commission asserts that, "there is a public interest in the unborn at all stages,"[1] and recommends creation of a general crime of foetal destruction or harm, with an exception for abortions carried out with medical authorization in three circumstances: 1) during the first 22 weeks to protect the woman's physical or psychological health; 2) to save the woman's life or protect her against serious physical injury; 3) if the foetus is suffering from a disability of such severity that medical treatment could be legally withheld upon its birth.

The initial focus on the foetus as a separate entity leads the Commission to a presumption that abortion is basically wrong, and the task then becomes carving

---

[1] *Crimes Against the Foetus*, p.43.

out a narrow range of exceptions as an acknowledgement of the interests of women at stake. These interests, however, are examined in a perfunctory way, in contrast with the careful consideration given to the central figure in the report, the foetus. The commission is dismissive of claims for abortion rights that are not based on protecting the life or health of the pregnancy woman, writing: "The notion that all human life has value argues against letting pure whim dictate termination of pregnancy. It opposes abortion done simply for capricious reasons."[1] The Commission energetically beats this straw person to the ground without ever addressing the actual claims for reproductive freedom or the realities of women's lives.

Limiting the availability of abortion, even at the earliest stages of pregnancy, to situations where the pregnant woman's life or health is threatened is one aspect of the state control recommended by the Commission. The requirement that every abortion be medically authorized is the second. The Commission never gives a reason for this restriction, except to say that criminal law must emphasize, "that pregnancy termination has to be—not least for the sake of the mother's own health—a medical matter."[2] The claim that it all for the pregnant woman's own good masks the assertion of state control implicit in effectively criminalizing "morning after" pills and other spontaneous abortifacients.

Technologies relating to abortion, contraception, and reproduction may enable women to achieve their goal of reproduction freedom. The state, however, is able to restrict this potential freedom through prohibitions and failure to provide services. Even women with unrestricted access to these technologies may be unable to control the terms of sex or reproduction in response to which technologies have been created. Pro-active negotiation of the terms—the ideology—surrounding sex and reproduction, is crucially important if we are to develop technologies that promote reproductive freedom. In the words of Barbara Katz Rothman: "The ideology promotes the development of certain kinds of technology. If we start with a different way of thinking, we would have clearly different solutions."[3]

DR. M. J. BAILEY is Assistant Professor in the Faculty of Law, Queen's University, Kingston.

---

[1]
Crimes Against the Foetus, p.41. See also p.45.

[2]
Crimes Against the Foetus, p.47.

[3]
"Toward the Future: Feminism and Reproductive Technologies," (1988/89) 37: 1 *Buffalo Law Review* 203 at p.226.

17

John R. de la Mothe

Regulation and Pervasive Technology

It is quite clear that, in our time, technology *has* become pervasive. Of this there is no doubt. Nor should there be any doubt of the profound importance of this. Indeed, as C.P. Snow rightly pointed out nearly fifty years ago, science and technology have not only been responsible for changing our perceptions of our natural and "selected" environments[1] but, they have also been responsible for fundamentally changing our perceptions of ourselves (as individuals and as members of humanity).[2] Thus it is perfectly fair, in my view, to extend these observations to claim—as George Grant, Jacob Bronowski, and many others have—that ours is a technological condition, that every waking moment of our existence is shaped or in some way mediated by technology.[3] However, when I am pressed to move beyond this powerful, if tacit, understanding in order to consider the relationship between technology and regulation—and more particularly, when I am brought to wonder if it is fair to expect or to hope for a pervasive

---

[1] Within the category of "selected" environments, we can easily include:

(a) *work environments* which now regularly feature personal computers (PCs) and word processors, optical scanners, FAX machines, numerically controlled machine tools, assembly lines, or industrial robots,

(b) *corporate environments* which feature real-time ultra-fast computing and networking facilities, cellular telephones, and private (on-call) jets,

(c) *home environments* which feature microwave ovens and self-cleaning ovens, video cassette players (VCRs), smoke detectors, colour televisions, self-timed coffee machines with alarm clocks, and telephones from which we can call almost anywhere in the world without the assistance of an operator,

(d) *urban environments* which feature technological mazes ranging from neon lights, subways systems, and apartment buildings with heat-sensing technology attuned to track burglars. So well adapted is the modern urbanscape that it even offers the pretence of escape through suburbs.

[2] Here, Snow was referring principally to our move away from a anthropocentric view of the universe to a heliocentric view, but the impact that science and technology have had on values has been equally profound. The realization that ours is a technological condition in fact offers us the exciting opportunity of constantly reconsidering our relationship with others, our notions of "liberty," and so on.

[3] I hope it is clear that when I say "technology" I am also referring to science and research which is carried out within the science system.

system of regulation to protect us from an "equally" pervasive technology—then I am compelled to briefly remind myself of a series of fundamental but crucial caveats which are needed to avoid being swayed by dystopian, anti-technology arguments which have little practical value.[1]

First, before we—as law makers, public policy makers, academicians, or citizens—begin to consider how to protect individuals and our society from the negative impacts of technology, we must attempt to realistically understand the character of technology, risk, and public policy.

Second, in so doing we must expect that—in the future—technology is going to become only more pervasive, not less. Evidence supporting this view is before us on a daily basis. For example, technology is becoming widely recognized as being increasingly important to both the social well-being and the economic competitiveness of nations, regions and firms. As a result, business leaders, economists and international agencies such as the Organisation for Economic Cooperation and Development (OECD) are beginning to talk of technologies" pervasiveness in terms of "embedded" technology and the "invisible" investment in R&D. If one thing can be discerned from all this so-called neo-technology or "new wave" economics, it is that we can no longer usefully speak—except at the most abstract levels—of "Technology." "Technology"—as a macro-concept—can only exist at the level of political theory. At the far more practical level of public policy making, risk and regulation, there can never be "Technology"—instead there can only be a vast array of complex and discrete (yet interacting) systems which we can identify as individual "technologies." Each of these technologies features fairly unique rates of diffusion, trajectories, and so on. Thus, once we understand the pluralism of technologies, we can then be more articulate about what we mean when we speak of those aspects of "pervasive technology" which—we deem—require regulation.

Of course, working with a more disaggregated view of technology does not, in any way, remove the ethical dimension from technology. Indeed, it places the burden of ethics squarely onto everyone involved in its development and use (including consumers). Even at this level, technologies, which could be defined as a family of methods used for associating and channelling other entities and forces (both human and non-human), naturally embody ethics (as much as the mathematician would like to deny any involvement in deaths caused by a weapons system which he or she helped to develop). This is so, quite simply, because at every discrete stage of the R&D chain (research—development—design—testing—commercialization—and, on the part of the consumer, purchase) there is an individual ethical choice in what to do next.

Third, we must understand that we can never know all of the risks we will face in a technology—either in developing it, deploying it or long after it has become part of our environment. As a result, we can never possibly regulate against Technology. To do so would not only remove any of the day-to-day freedoms which we gain through the use of technologies, but we would also lose any

---

[1] In the comments that follow, I will refrain from considering pervasive regulation as a deliberately oppressive intervention into the lives of a nation's citizenry. Instead, I will restrict myself to a consideration of more selective intervention on behalf of genuine public protection.

measure of what it means to be free. If we are to retain a vibrant, creative and open society, we can only develop (as we have in many instances) screening mechanisms through which to minimize risk prior to exposing ourselves to a new technology or technological product, and we can only effectively regulate against future risks in a *post hoc* fashion.

At first glance, this observation may not seem to give much in the way of comfort for those who are anxious to regulate all of the negative aspects of pervasive technology. Indeed it would seem, in some way, to support the widespread perception that the dangers of living in a technological world are increasing. But we must understand that the vast majority of technology is by no means riskier—either to our physical well being or to our rights and freedoms—than the technologies we have deployed in the past. It would be wrong to indict elevators or the entire pharmaceutical industry because people have died as a result of malfunctioning elevators or because of a patient's unexpected reaction to medication. Instead, the deeper problem is that our level of fear has increased—fuelling our common perception that technologies are riskier—(a) as technologies have become more pervasive,[1] (b) as technologies interact for the first time in routine ways (as with electronic controls in airliners)—and fail, and (c) as technologies, which we are on the verge of developing, force us, uncomfortably, to re-consider what it means to be human. In vitro fertilization and electronic customer cards which scan our bank accounts and immediately withdraw the total amount at the point of purchase all present us with a vast range of opportunities which would have been unthinkable—except in science fiction—earlier in our lives. But, when we accept the newfound options we also accept the potential risk which each new option embodies. This is something of a truism, of course. But if we were to comprehensively think about the character of risk, one would realize—as Mary Douglas and Aaron Wilsavsky have—that risks are hidden, that risks are selected, and that risks are perceived. Risks are not absolute.[2] And thus, any regulation which tried to be pervasive would only succeed in eliminating freedoms and would not remove any appreciable amount of risk from technology.

Fourth, we must understand that despite the profound impact which science and technology are having on every aspect of the public sphere, the interface between science, technology and public policy is very rarely well-defined. This apparent paradox is attributable to a number of factors, prominent among which are questions relating to the nature of scientific uncertainty and the limits of the public policy process. As an example of this, let us take the case of acid rain. We can begin with the now widely understood proposition of the acid rain debate: that sulphur dioxide and oxides of nitrogen released from factory smokestacks and motorized vehicles are responsible for the creation of acid depositions. From this view flows the seemingly reasonable assertion that stricter controls of these pollutants would take care of the acid rain problem. However this is precisely

---

[1]

Humans have always had a natural predilection to fear that which cannot be seen or easily understood.

[2]

Mary Douglas and Aaron Wildavsky, *Risk and Culture*, (Berkeley: University of California Press, 1982).

where questions of scientific uncertainty and the limits of the policy process become problematic.

Policy-makers assume that because scientists cannot identify specific sources as causing specific increases in acid depositions, they also cannot make relevant statements about general principles of acid deposition. This is obviously not true. The problems undermining the politicians' ability to assess scientific findings include "Do they understand the problem?"; "Can they assess the significance of scientific results?"; "What interests (values) are motivating their choice of facts in searching for solutions?"; "How will their actions be viewed by political allies and enemies, and by voters?" ... An example of this sort of uncertainty is the inability of some policy-makers to agree on such facts as the likely increase in emissions that might result from an economic recovery.

However, the flow of uncertainty between scientists and policy-makers runs in both directions. Scientists often have difficulty understanding the political uncertainties that are imposed on the analysis process. In the case of the U.S./Canada bilateral Memorandum of Intent on acid rain, the disclaimers added by the U.S. delegates made it difficult for scientists to understand their role. If, as some scientists felt, political considerations would overrule their work, then how could they contribute to the policy debate?

These uncertainties have varying sources. Some stem from the inherent human subjectivity of scientific analysis. As well, economic interests tend to emphasize different aspects of uncertainty, while further uncertainty seems to arise from uncertainty itself. Nevertheless, within such policy debates in which technology is necessarily implied, value decisions and politics will often enter into the equation while masquerading as scientific uncertainty. Regardless of how right or wrong such behaviour may seem, decisions for future action (such as policy) can never be objectively grounded, just—as we have already seen—they can not be ethically neutral.

Thus, in sum, in considering what types of regulation can or should be expected in an age of pervasive technology, certain pointers should be clear.

- For practical and effective regulations, technology can never be considered as a macro-concept. It can only be dealt with at a fairly disaggregated level.
- Risks from technology are hidden, selected and largely perceived.
- The public policy process in an open society cannot conceive of, or deliver, anything resembling a pervasive regulation against technology.

And perhaps most important,

- Ethical choice—in technology, regulation, and public policy—always rests with individuals—including ourselves. They always rest in our decisions as to what to do next. By considering the individual character of technologies, our age may usefully force us to carefully re-articulate the individual values which we need in a technological world. In so doing, technology may yet encourage us to find our pervasive regulation within ourselves.

DR. J.R. DE LA MOTHE is Vice Chairman, International Science Policy Foundation, Graduate Faculty of Administration at the University of Ottawa.

UNIT VII
CULTURE, LEARNING, AND ACCESSIBILITY

18

John Meisel

Innovation in Communication and the Media: Social and Ethical Issues

Even a shameless braggart, wildly overstating the implications of new technologies and their capability to create, store, transmit and retrieve information, could not exaggerate their social and ethical importance. It is no whit less critical than the ethics of bio-engineering. Two reasons account for the pivotal place occupied by information technology in the scheme of things. In the first place, it affects the minds of individuals by shaping their perceptions, attitudes, thoughts, and values. We are what the information we receive makes us. And the content of this information cannot be divorced from the means used to create and transmit it. The mode of communication, whether it be a mother's caress, speech, eye contact, a letter, a quick scribble, a computer printout, sky-writing or a television program, colours the substance of what is transmitted, received, and digested. The medium, as the eminent Marshall McLuhan said in another context, truly is the message.

Secondly, there is a good deal of evidence that the way in which people exchange information—the technology of communication, in other words—actually affects the way in which the brain functions. The extent to which individuals use the left and/or right hemisphere of the brain may be determined by the form in which knowledge reaches them. Reading something on a solidly printed written page, for instance, may involve a different mental process than gazing at the ephemeral image appearing on a computer screen.

Before identifying some of the social and ethical issues arising from the new technologies, we must briefly note the areas of life affected by them. The fusion of highly sophisticated computers with revolutionary communications technologies, like fibre optics and satellite transmission, dramatic miniaturization of equipment (microchips, for instance), advanced switching processes in telephony, or the widespread use of videotapes and VCRs, have fundamentally altered three vitally important aspects of everyone's work and leisure. Telecommunications—the electronic exchange of voice messages, data or images—affect the way we do our banking, pay our bills, protect our homes, send documents, among many other things, and also how and where we store business, industrial, governmental and personal information. Secondly, innovation in the production, delivery and reproduction of radio and, particularly, television programs has created a revolution in entertainment habits. Finally, cultural life—music, painting, holography, performing arts, desk-top publishing, for instance—are assuming forms which would have astounded and probably shocked those whose names are hallowed among the major creative geniuses of the world.

Of the immense number of social and ethical issues presented by the new information technology, a few stand out as particularly challenging. The first to be considered here arises from the fact that the new technologies are likely to widen the gap between the rich and the poor, between those benefitting immensely from the new gadgetry and those deriving little or no direct advantage from it. The chasm appears at two levels—the personal and the international. In the latter case, the rich, highly developed, scientifically sophisticated countries are outpacing, even more than heretofore, the less favoured states. This is already manifest at the economic, cultural, educational, and medical levels, among many others. In the area of communications, particularly, the younger, weaker countries are threatened by a massive barrage of information which they are unprepared to assimilate or counter.[1]

Insofar as individuals are concerned, there are the computer literate people and those who are ill at ease in the presence of the constantly changing hardware and software. Many other factors, such as geographical proximity, institutional links, financial resources, also determine the degree of access a particular person has to the enormously enriching information stored in data banks. The presence, in society, of information-rich and information-poor people exacerbates already long-standing inequalities. The difficult problem arises when considering what might be done to ensure that the benefits of the new technology are spread reasonably evenly so that social cohesion is strengthened rather than weakened.

A second knotty issue of our new age concerns the seemingly paradoxical fact that new technology on the one hand draws all parts of the world closer together, while at the same time strengthening the ties to the particular and the local. Central data banks now store in one place vitally important information derived from all over the world. Thus a foreign-owned Canadian company, say, in the automobile sector, may find that records critical to its operations are "deposited" in the United States. This means that the manner in which the information is organized and possibly even gathered must conform to standards which may have little to do with conditions prevailing in Canada. Similarly, television programs now cater to world audiences. A show like *Dallas* or *Dynasty* is followed avidly on several continents and in scores of languages. Programming and program tastes are becoming international and are, of course, dominated by the immense strength of the United States TV industry. The reasons for this are complex but are, to a very great extent, related to economics and market factors, as well as to the nature of American popular culture. (Similarly, McDonald's golden arches now flourish in France, Mexico and Russia.) Under these circumstances, people's reference points, their choice of entertainment and preoccupations cease, in part, to be rooted in their own society. This homogenizes the world and tends to sap the creative vitality that comes from diversity.

---

[1] The International Commission for the Study of Communications Problems, *Many Voices, One World*, The McBride Report, (London: Kogan Page, 1980).

On the other hand, this same phenomenon increases, to some extent, the shared experiences of countries and may weaken parochialism—no bad thing. Widespread, cross-national collaboration has been increased dramatically. Thus, the stunning new edition of the *Oxford English Dictionary* was produced in a surprisingly short time by lexicographers who were in Oxford while the keyboard operators were in Pennsylvania, the computer programmers in Waterloo, Ontario and in Britain, and the printers in Massachusetts.[1].

This many-stranded global web, however, also creates a need for people to maintain links with their own communities. Thus, the "nationalization" of newspapers—the phenomenon of *USA Today*, for instance, or the ubiquitous availability of national editions of papers like the Toronto *Globe and Mail* and the *New York Times*, is accompanied by the unprecedented flourishing of neighbourhood publications that carry personal ads, report the loss of cats and provide advertising geared to highly local markets.

Technology itself facilitates the production of goods and services centred on small, particular (as distinct from universal) markets. This is perfectly exemplified in desk top publishing which has made it possible for "boutique" publishers to compete quite effectively with the giants, thus assisting local and regional writers and challenging the monopolistic trends evident in the growing number of multinational media conglomerates.

Governments and individuals are compelled, by the tendencies just described, to determine what policies and actions are needed to cope with their consequences and how to harmonize them into a satisfying equilibrium. The issues are complex and raise a whole host of questions about the nature of communities, the autonomy of regions or ethnic groups, fair standards of distribution, and so on.

A third area that presents us with fascinating and important problems concerns the extent to which the new information technology can invade privacy and tear down the cloak which used to protect men and women against unwanted intrusion. Manifestations of this real or potential snooping are numerous, but none is more threatening than the information being assembled about individuals in various data banks. Governments, banks, sales organizations, entertainment and travel booking agencies, hotels, cable companies, home security firms, medical establishments, insurance houses, and many others, accumulate information about citizens and customers which are stored in their data bases. It is now quite possible, particularly in light of the expanding use of social insurance numbers, to collate much or all of this information for any given person and to obtain from it a detailed and intimate portrait of the individual concerned. Although it is true that considerable efforts are made to protect these data from unauthorized eyes and to safeguard confidentiality, instances exist of highly sensitive information, including income tax records, finding their way into unauthorized hands. Computer crime is rising, and governments, particularly in the guise of police forces and espionage or counter-espionage agents, have shown little reticence about obtaining personal information when they deem that the national interest (as defined by them, of

---

[1] Araminta Wordsworth, "The Oxford Goes High-Tech," *The Financial Post*, (April 22–24, 1989), pp.1,7.

course) demands it. The record of the FBI, the CIA, and even of the RCMP, is not reassuring in this regard.

The advantages of storing information by means of computer technology are such that we can now no longer do without it. But means have to be devised to protect individuals from the pitfalls associated with the process. The ethics of information provision, storing and withdrawal requires careful and urgent attention.[1]

The application of what has been called "compunications"—the linking of computers and the new telecommunications—to politics presents us with a fourth area that raises serious ethical challenges. The new electronic wizardry has made constant and instantly reported polling commonplace. It has also made it possible to consult citizens' opinions through plebiscites using interactive cable services.

Other technological developments, such as the light, miniaturized video camera, have dramatically altered the manner in which media and politics interact. The economics of TV demands that the medium deliver the maximum number of viewers to advertisers. This has led to a ubiquitous reliance on news clips and a heavy emphasis on party leaders and on "personalities" rather than on issues. Thus, party leaders must now be telegenic and campaigns must be managed by professional media consultants, who usurp much of the role formerly played by party volunteers. The so-called leaders' debates can decide an election, and the organization of major political events (like leadership conventions) is arranged to suit the priorities of television programming.

These are only some of the features of the "new politics" forged by the information revolution, which pose endless problems not only of political management but also of ethics. Although we cannot explore them here, we can illustrate some of their dimensions by looking to one issue that has caused much debate: the use of public opinion polls. How appropriate is it for endless numbers of polls to bombard the public, often without specifying precisely how they were made and how the data are interpreted. Have the polls fanned the tendency of the media to resort to "horse race" election coverage—that is, the tendency to dwell almost exclusively on the question of who is ahead at the expense of substance: party programs or the competence of candidates? Should these examinations of the public pulse be banned during the week or so prior to election day? Would it be in the public interest to have polls conducted by disinterested agencies like the Chief Electoral Officer or Statistics Canada, rather than by commercial firms or the media themselves? Do polls help or hinder the best translation of the public's judgement about public issues into its electoral choice? What, if anything, can be done about these problems without interfering with freedom of speech and expression? Is it desirable to regulate polling in our society? If so, how?

And what about private polls—the daily sweeps done by the parties which attempt to penetrate the innermost psyche of the electorate? Modern technology makes it possible to have a thorough and reliable analysis of the reaction to a

---

[1]

For additional information, see David H. Flaherty (ed.), *Privacy and Data Protection: An International Bibliography*, (London: Mansell, 1984), and David H. Flaherty, *Protecting Privacy in Two-Way Electronic Services*, (White Plains: Knowledge Industry Publications, Inc. 1985).

leader's speech practically within minutes of its delivery. Does this distort the political process? Are leaders and their legion of advisers irresistibly tempted to give the public what they think it wants to hear rather than what they believe should be done?

While some of these and similar conundrums existed before the current innovations in information technology, they have assumed new and much more pressing forms as a result of it.

Finally, in our sampler of social and ethical problems of the information age, we shall consider its impact on a couple of everyday aspects of modern life. Although our examples may seem trivial, they show that the effect of new technologies can have a deep impact on the individual. Take the seemingly inconsequential problem of noise as exemplified by universally diffused music. It is now impossible to escape the constant bombardment of penetrating noise. Beaches, street corners, factories, elevators, waiting rooms, dentists' offices, buses, even telephone lines while one is "on hold," are filled with Muzak or the latest hits which may or may not be welcome. Some people no doubt enjoy the din, but others might prefer Mozart, and still others, silence. Sound technology has shattered silence and has invaded the lives of hapless prisoners of din. Among the issues raised by this feature of modern life is the question of whether the rights of those who like to be left alone, who prefer to escape the decibel assault, should be honoured. A more consequential matter concerns the growing use of videocasettes, teleshopping, telemarketing, teleconferencing and telelearning—in short, of teleliving. One consequence of this unquestionably convenient trend is that many people leave home less frequently and so miss some of the stimulation of moving in a wider world, of enjoying unexpected encounters or of complementing one set of activities with all manner of social contacts which provide important variety and personal enrichment. It is a little too soon to say how extensive the electronically induced narrowing of human experience is becoming as the result of breakthroughs in telephony, but the slower than expected espousal of teleshopping and of interactive cable suggests that some important social needs are being neglected by those who choose telephonic communication at the expense of more traditional encounters.

As in almost all the areas we have discussed, however, there can be little doubt that the convenience, efficiency and flexibility of the new ways is also intensely satisfying. Some important needs are met by the new services; those of the handicapped, for instance. Electronic mail and computer networking have aided research, business and, yes, have also added a great deal of pleasure to the lives of countless numbers of people.

The lesson from all this is, of course, that we have to learn to use technology wisely. We must find the proper mix of new and old, and we must be alert to the ethical, social, and psychological consequences of technological change so as to accrue the undoubted benefits while avoiding the drawbacks. In this way we will control the effects of technology. Otherwise they will control us.

DR. J. MEISEL is Professor in Political Studies at Queen's University, Kingston, Ontario.

19   *Clive Beck*

Technology and Education: An Ethical Perspective

One key ethical question in education is to what extent we should *use* technology in teaching and learning. Some people maintain that educational technology inevitably has a dehumanizing effect on learners; and others see it as biasing learners (and teachers) toward the values of the military-industrial complex, so closely associated with the rise of technology.

Another question has to do with *content* of education. How much time should be spent on initiation *into* technology and how much on learning *about* technology and other aspects of personal and societal life. In more specific areas we should be looking at what should be taught, for example, about the impact of technology on the "quality of life," the effects of technology on the local and global environment, the pitfalls of introducing technology from "developed" countries into "underdeveloped" countries and the possibilities and dangers of the new reproductive technologies?

Underscoring these issues is the fact that technologies are not only "gadgets" or "machines" of R&D but should also be understood as being part of the culture and social know-how of a society that drives R&D. The latter as "soft" technologies cannot be separated from the former as "hard" technologies. Therefore, education in itself is a technology, i.e. a social technology while the art of teaching and teaching methods are techniques[1] of education. As social technologies have a distinctly cultural and ideological make-up, they are inherently value-laden bringing with them their own ethical concerns and implications.

To begin on a positive note, information technology offers, I believe, great opportunities for increasing the general level of education in the world. Newspapers, magazines, mass market books, radio, TV, film, videos, multimedia packages, computer assisted learning, computerized information retrieval, instruction and dialogue by telephone and cable TV, all of these are having an enormous educational impact. While many of the messages broadcast through the mass media take the form of propaganda or simple entertainment, a great deal of dissemination of valuable information and concepts occurs, placing people in a better position to make sound value decisions.

In addition to information, the mass media offer extensive discussion of ethical issues. In recent months alone, the world news media have commented at length on the greenhouse effect, damage to the ozone layer, acid rain, oil pollution at sea, depletion of rain forests, the arms build-up, nuclear energy, artificial reproduction,

---
[1] Jacques Ellul, *The Technological Society*, (New York: Vintage Books, 1964), p.xxv.

abortion, organ transplantation, free-trade, monetary policy, socialism versus capitalism, continued imperialism, repressive regimes in various countries, treatment of native peoples, and poverty and starvation around the world. Information of this type, despite its biases, constitutes a major form of ethical education, probably far outstripping what is currently done in formal education programmes.

Debates among philosophers rage back and forth about the foundations of ethics. We are all affected by the consequences of our actions and as such, it seems inescapable that ethical behaviour, as far as possible, take account of the consequences of those very actions. With improved information technology and the individual and societal acquisition of knowledge, comes responsibility, that is the responsibility to act ethically in individual, national and global terms. Not to take advantage of this capability would, I believe, show a lack of ethical responsibility.

The rapid growth of dissemination of information and ideas *outside* formal education calls for a shift in emphasis in educational theory and practice. Educators must become involved in informal education, developing parallel "curricula," learning materials and teaching strategies for both types of setting. If something is worth teaching, it is worth teaching in and out of school. Also, a major activity in formal education must be the examination and critique of the information and ideas being passed on through new technologies. For example, students in school should have programmes in television appreciation and criticism; and as well as learning how to access encyclopedias on personal computers, they should also become familiar with how such knowledge bases are created and understand the pressures—economic, ideological, political—which can lead to biased content.

The foregoing discussion of educational technology clearly assumes that technology is not always bad. On the other hand, at least one major theorist of contemporary society—Jacques Ellul—has claimed that it *is* always bad. In *The Technological Society*, Ellul maintains that society is becoming overwhelmed by technique in a way that "presents man [sic] with multiple problems." [1] The term *technique*, as used by Ellul, "does not mean machines, technology, or that and that procedure for attaining an end," although these are included. Rather, it refers to *"the totality of methods rationally arrived at and having absolute efficiency* (for a given stage of development) in *every* field of human activity." [2] The pervasiveness of technology in the modern world, according to Ellul, is having disastrous consequences for humankind. The new technological order "was meant to be a buffer between man and nature. Unfortunately, it has evolved autonomously in such a way that man has lost all contact with his natural framework...he cannot pierce the shell of technology to find again the ancient milieu to which he was adapted for hundreds of thousands of years." [3]

However, in my view, it is not technique as such which is the problem but the *misuse* of technique. Even Ellul proposes a technique for achieving the key human

---

[1]
  Ibid., p.xxxii.
[2]
  Ibid., p.xxv.
[3]
  Ibid., p.428.

values he identifies. He says in a nutshell: Do not spend time trying to change modern society (it is futile), do not compromise with our technology-infested society, assert your individuality, and opt for freedom, justice and truth.[1] But this is in principle no different from the technologies Ellul rejects: it is proposed (mistakenly, I believe) as an effective way of achieving true human values. Clearly we must employ technique; for if we regard certain things as valuable for human beings, it would not make sense—indeed, it would be unethical—not to pursue them in an effective manner. It is sometimes suggested that the best way to achieve certain ends—happiness and other people's respect, for example—is not to pursue them directly but at most to hope for them as a by-product of other activities. However, even this is a technique (again, not a very wise one, I believe) for attaining these ends.

Of course, *exclusive* concentration on method or technique is an evil, one which is widespread in contemporary society. We are often so preoccupied with means that we lose sight of the ends, the basic values that make life worthwhile. As Alasdair MacIntyre has said, our "utilitarian" approach to life has gone so far that "one goes to primary school in order to get a degree in order to get a job in order to rise in one's profession in order to get a pension."[2] Ellul has done us a service in drawing attention to aspects of this problem. But he has greatly overstated his case. The solution lies not in rejecting technology but in finding *appropriate* technologies for society in general and more specifically for education and giving them *due* emphasis. Indeed, if we tried to turn away from technique, it would bind us ever more firmly. Paradoxically, we must develop techniques for keeping technique in its proper place in our thought and behaviour. Technophobia, like many other phobias, is ultimately self-defeating.

Having said all this, however, we must acknowledge that the use of technology has *in fact* run amuck in a number of specific areas. In educational method, for example, we often feel we must use certain technologies—such as audiovisual materials, computer assisted instruction, values clarification techniques—simply because they are there, without a clear sense of what will be accomplished. Also, we often assume that something worthwhile is going on simply because a set of educational technologies are being applied, even when this is not the case. Ivan Illich has pointed out that the institution of schooling has become an end in itself, a "false public utility," a credentials factory, and just as "medical care is mistaken for health care (and) social work for improvement of community life," so schooling is mistaken for education.[3] Further, in our preoccupation with the technology of schooling, we often lose sight of the students. Schooling becomes dehumanizing—a set of techniques applied to someone; human relationships are not fostered and human concerns are forgotten.

Going beyond educational method to *content*, we find huge areas of neglect and/or miseducation. For example, the phenomena of "modernity" and "develop-

---

[1]
  Ibid.

[2]
  Alasdair MacIntyre, "Against Utilitarianism," in T.H.B. Hollins (ed.), *Aims in Education: The Philosophic Approach*, (Manchester: The University of Manchester Press, 1964), p.1.

[3]
  Ivan Illich, *Deschooling Society*, (New York: Harper & Row, 1971), p.1.

ment" are inadequately studied. It is frequently assumed in schools, universities and informal adult teaching programmes that to be "modern" is better than to be traditional—the former being viewed as progressive while the latter is viewed as being conservative—and that "development" is clearly an advantage. The cultural underpinnings of these terms are rarely understood and the ethical implications of "who benefits" even less so. There is need for systematic study of these concepts and of the price that is paid for technological development in the so-called "developed" world. There is also a need to educate the "developed" world of the ways in which "development" in industrialized nations is achieved at the expense of Third World countries, and about the great harm that is often done by exporting expensive and inappropriate technologies to these regions.

There is also inadequate study of environmental issues. In particular, insufficient attention is given to the ecological side effects of various technologies, both locally and around the globe. People should learn how to estimate the *full cost* of technological "advances" in terms of both resource depletion and environmental damage. Study is needed of phenomena such as the greenhouse effect, damage to the ozone layer, and the introduction of poisons into food and drinking water, all of which may be traced in large measure to technological "progress."

Focusing on the human environment in a narrower sense, there should be extensive study in educational settings of the *effects* of technology on the daily "quality of life." Here, of course, the picture is mixed: on the positive side, labour-saving devices such as washing machines, dishwashers, ploughs and windmills reduce the burden of tedious, back-breaking work; and on the negative side, stresses and strains are often imposed by technology on individuals and groups. However, too often the latter are not studied, and so the full balance-sheet is not revealed. The various technologies need to be assessed not only in terms of their advantages but also, for example, in terms of air pollution, noise pollution, light pollution, aesthetic damage, nervous strain and, last but not least, monetary cost. Some technologies are so expensive simply from a financial point of view that people have to work harder and harder to pay for them. This is true in the Third World where, as Gustavo Esteva says, "that is what economic development is all about: to impose work on the people."[1] However, it is true also in wealthy countries where hours of work, especially for women but also for men, have, if anything, been on the increase in recent years. We must keep asking: does this or that technology, on balance, increase or decrease the quality of our lives and at what expense in both capital and non-capital terms?

To take an even more specific example, there is need for extensive study of reproductive technologies. Sexuality and reproduction are major areas of human concern. Fiction, non-fiction, film, television, gossip columns, counselling programs and everyday conversations touch on them constantly. And yet formal educational enterprises give them such inadequate attention. The shortcomings of traditional "sex education" are well known: too few topics are dealt with too briefly and too mechanically. But there is also almost complete neglect of the new reproductive technologies such as artificial conception, genetic engineering, and

---

[1] Gustevo Esteva, "A New Call for Celebration," *Development: Seeds of Change*, Vol. 3 (1986), p.97.

pre-natal testing for gender and abnormalities. These technologies raise enormous ethical questions which education has a responsibility to address.

Part of the problem of education today is that so much time is taken up with *initiation into* technologies and the technological way of life while so little is devoted to the *study* of issues of technology and contemporary life of the kind reviewed above. Education is seen too much in terms of unreflective vocational preparation—whether for professional or non-professional jobs—and not enough in terms of personal and social enhancement. There is need for a major shift in the focus of educational enterprises. One difficulty is that the curriculum of schools and universities is cluttered with traditional studies and make-work activities of less than optimal value. But more importantly, we so often do not even see the *need* for the systematic study of fields such as politics, economics, culture, ecology and personal and social values. It seems to be assumed that insights in these areas are to come to us "naturally" or "intuitively" or through the application of a handful of moral principles learned at our parents' knees or in the local temple (important though these learning are). In fact, the world today is so complex, interdependent and changeable that it is extremely difficult to learn how to live well, personally, and socially, without extensive education of both a formal and an informal kind.

Part of what is being proposed here is a more "spiritual" approach to education. Both the method and the content of education must take account of the full range of human values, and not merely the technological values. In the emerging "global village," we must go beyond being mere users and consumers of technology learning to live the "good life" in material terms and develop as human beings in more holistic terms. Therefore, we must cultivate spiritual values essential to that good life, such as awareness, integration, wonder, hope, aesthetic appreciation, concern for others and the environment, love and gentleness. We must learn to construct a social and economic order within which it is possible, despite our human limitations, to have and express spiritual virtues. Within such a humane, spiritual order, technology has a major place. But, as was noted earlier, we must ensure that the technology is *appropriate* and the emphasis placed on it is neither too little nor too great. For this, we require (among other things) a very broad education with a strong values emphasis which will help us make sound ethical choices with respect to technology.

DR. CLIVE BECK is Professor of Philosophy at OISE (Ontario Institute for Studies in Education), University of Toronto.

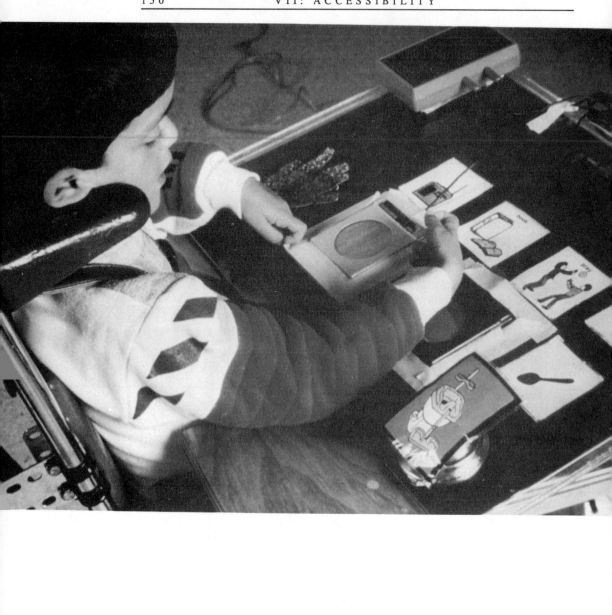

20   *J.C.M. Shute*

Technology and Human Resource Development

To many discussions and analyses of technology, like technology itself, seem to take place in a vacuum as if technologies could somehow be understood without reference to the social, political, economic and biological context in which they inevitably and invariably function. One current exception to this dismal tendency is the search for benevolent links between technology and a sustainable biosphere in which all non-human organisms can somehow exist in harmony with humanity's primordial urge to dominate, transform, subdue and consume virtually every element in the natural order. The assumption appears to be that harmony is possible, that human beings can, by modifying these primordial behaviours, return our small planet to a state approaching equilibrium. There are, however, those who would view such an assumption as naive in the extreme and who would prescribe only the most drastic reforms if the human family is to persist as a species into the foreseeable future. And so our concern for the natural environment on which all planetary life depends, although excessively delayed, is finally growing and becoming an issue of relevance.

Nonetheless, such genuine concern for the global environment and such fragmented political action as we can detect do not pay sufficient heed to either the social costs or the social impacts of a variety of technologies, some of which are outright malevolent. It is as if the politicians, planners and pundits find solutions to all the pressing problems of the day in the application of ever more technology. Perhaps the excessive disciplinary orientation of most training and education is partly to blame for narrow, pigeon-holed attitudes. Politicians negotiate purely political decisions (or lack of them); economists seek re-structuring and resource re-allocation; agricultural scientists search for more efficient practices; ecologists criticize the others and call for genuine respect for the integrity and unity of the natural world. Who, then, is the advocate for amorphous humanity, the latter being the subject and object of technological systems of every bewildering type while both the victim and the beneficiary of every idea, technique, device and instrumentality which the scientist, the engineer, the technologist and the entrepreneur can invent and market?

On the other hand, one needs to be reminded of the resilient capabilities of persons to create, modify, reform, adapt and even subvert technology. In our time in history, the imperative to exert control over technology is more urgent, than in past periods. And so to build up the stock of appropriate human skills, particularly in ways that are relevant to the awesome demands of our time, both to equip the powerless with a critical voice and to attain new heights of creative problem-solving, is a task of supreme urgency. The mechanisms for doing so are, sadly, never addressed by those concerned with mindlessly marketing new technologies nor by those seeking solutions in technology alone. Even some enlightened environmentalists appear blinkered by their perceptions. In the universities, for instance, there are those who purport to teach sustainable development without reference to human beings. In major global statements on development and environment, however enlightened otherwise, like the Brandt Report, the Brundtland Commission Report or the Bogeve Declaration, means of marshalling human skills and ability are virtually ignored. Something is askew in our equations, our definitions and the plans that emerge from them. That something is the absence of adequate and concerted attention to human resource development.

What is Human Resource Development?

Probably because of their preoccupation with the allocation of resources, economists have had the most to say about human resource development (HRD), and this fact alone accounts for much of the semantic fuzziness associated with the term. For most economists and planners, a resource is something that is identified, acquired, processed and transformed into something else of commercial or utilitarian value. It is an input into the industrial processing sequence; its value related entirely to its further use at a later stage of processing or in its end-use as an item of consumption. Thus, labelling human beings as "resources" runs the risk, in this utilitarian view, of treating people as disembodied factors of production rather than as flesh and blood creatures of infinite variety existing as individuals, groups and communities in every society. However, the fact that some planners, economists and other technocrats have drawn attention to HRD is doubtless salutary, as it has reminded the rest of us that modernization is both the product of human ingenuity and the cause of much human and environmental stress.

How, then, should HRD be defined? It seems to me that a critical ethical distinction, not merely a working definition, rides on the answer. If HRD is defined only as an instrument for building up the stock of labour and management skills for purposes of increasing output, income and wealth, then one is not so open to conceptions of HRD that place the person, rather than the process or the outcome, at the centre, that permit individual, group and community aspiration and creativity to come before production and wealth generation. In case the reader feels that I am making an artificial distinction, I need only point to the frightful social consequences of historical investments in capital-intensive technologies dependent on expendable human "inputs," from the nineteenth century Industrial Revolution to the present-day computer, robotics and "smart" technology revolution.

Traditionally, HRD has been synonymous with education and training aimed at providing people with skills and attitudes appropriate to life in industrialized societies. More recently, management has been added to the HRD family. Among the cousins are institutional strengthening, technology transfer, innovation, community development, communication, and non-formal education. The underlying assumption is that all of these elements of HRD presuppose basic literacy and numeracy. Thus, literacy training is a prominent (and usually unquestioned) element in most HRD strategies in the Third World and increasingly part of HRD in industrialized countries, some of whose citizens have encountered difficulties in completing formal schooling.

The mechanistic view of HRD evolved largely from several observations. Following World War II, it was felt that the Marshall Plan for European reconstruction could be replicated in tropical dependencies approaching independence. Rather abruptly, this shallow assumption was tempered by the discovery that as well as capital and infrastructure, skills are essential in national development. This "human capital" concept gained strength from subsequent observations that investment in formal education yielded high returns in lifetime earnings and that such investment brought even higher returns than investment in physical capital, especially in developing countries. Though these correlations were challenged by sociologists and others, the generality applies that investment in education, training and attendant HRD components are highly correlated to literacy levels, health indicators, income, upward mobility, status, infant and child mortality and life expectancy. Another clear correlation between HRD and technology arises in relation to the process of transferring technologies and their adoption by end-users. The higher the level of education/training, whether formal or non-formal, the greater the rate and extent of adoption of new ideas and techniques. This empirically demonstrable observation reinforces to some degree the propensity to see human beings as units in the production (technology application) process. Typically, it also bypasses or neglects the needs of the majority of the world's citizens who are less educated or illiterate, impoverished, isolated, rural and female. Is the ethical dilemma obvious? Apparently not, for the working assumption still appears to be that the natural and expected way of doing things is for technologies to be generated in the North and "transferred" to the South. It is true that Honda, Coca-Cola and military hardware provide outstanding examples of successful technology transfer. But in agriculture, health, communications and education, western transplants that do not accommodate indigenous values, techniques and approaches, have not worked well.

This last finding leads me to an inclusive definition of HRD, one which encompasses a range of measures designed not merely to inculcate skills for production or to induce some pre-ordained behavioural change, but to promote and sharpen a whole repertoire of humanizing attributes and to develop human capabilities. "Develop" as I use it means to "unfold" or "evolve" in contrast to its transitive connotation of imposition, exploitation and coercion. This conception of HRD includes, of course, all liberalizing forms of education, training, research, institutional management and strengthening, creativity and technology adaptation. My definition hinges on a worldview quite different, however, from that of the human capital theorist or garden-variety technocrat. For too long, in my opinion, rational, mechanistic, linear, Newtonian values have propelled us in the west. Not only have such values tied education (HRD) to an industrial/technological model but they have also proved to be in part destructive to humans and the fragile environment we inhabit. The obvious benefits derived from western technology, of course, should not by disparaged. Yet, the long-term consequences of this approach to technology and HRD are simply not sustainable and very possibly disastrous, as our capacity to make mistakes seems to outrun our willingness to correct them. What is needed, I would argue, is a shift in worldview that would foster an HRD strategy based on participatory and consultative approaches, respect for the enduring values and knowledge of non-western cultures, a greater degree of self-direction and autonomy, the cultivation of variability, the deliberate reduction of the urge to dominate, exploit and consume, and a willingness to learn from holistic and harmonious attitudes of the aboriginal and other groups so long scorned by hard-driving and aggressive western civilization.

Every nation and indeed many sub-sets within nations will, in this paradigm, need to make choices and find their own balance between powerful technologies and human aspirations. It looks to me though like an uphill battle to bring runaway technologies under the control of humane values. The pressing practical question for both public sector decision-makers and private sector managers is whether they will invest in technology, with only limited concern for the social and ecological consequences, or in human talent. All over the world, the demand for the latter is growing; it can be ignored or neglected, but only at very great social and environmental cost, as we have already begun to see.

DR. J.C.M. SHUTE is Professor of Rural Extension Studies at the University of Guelph.

Further Reading

Development, Special Issue on Education, (Ottawa: Canadian International Development Agency, 1985).

Worldscape, Special Issue on Human Resource Development. Fall, 1988, Vol 2, No.2, (Guelph: University of Guelph Centre for International Programs).

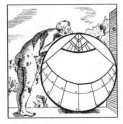

21   *Arun Abraham and James Mullin*

Beyond the Protocol: Ethics and Research for Development

C hin Keng-Wah was again confronted with a difficult situation. As a poor Asian farmer he has continually had to develop adaptive strategies for survival. Sufficient lowland is available to grow the rice which his family needs, and an additional 20 hectares of land has been devoted to sugarcane cultivation. The price of sugarcane is declining precipitously, so alternatives must be found. Cropping systems experiments have recently been conducted on similar upland areas. Rice, mungbean, maize, sorghum and tomatoes were the crops which had undergone field trials. Should he discontinue sugarcane cultivation and switch? If so, to which crop or set of crops? How will economic losses be mitigated should the newly developed crop varieties fail? Where will the onus for liability and compensation fall for the loss? Moreover, if he accepts the technology and the package of inputs which the local research institution has suggested, will he be, in essence, stepping onto a treadmill?

These are but a few of the questions which arise in situations common to the various types of externally-sponsored research in developing countries (LDCs). An African scientist has noted, in this connection, that the relevance of research, especially external, donor-funded research, for a given LDC should receive closer attention. "The host scientist might have accepted sponsorship because of lack of local funding or resources, even though the subject matter might not be of high priority for the community concerned."[1]

One observer comments that groups which are recipients of research and development support instigated by an external agent, regardless of the incentive, "are unlikely to have the cohesion, the internal thrust, or the drive to be more than passive actors in the development process."[2] Such a sweeping statement may not be necessarily true. It takes continuous, strenuous effort by donor agencies to prevent this from being the result. Taking a dominant position is an almost natural occurrence for a donor agency, which makes imperative the establishment of an ethic to ensure that it can never be characterized by the description in the above

---

[1]

S. Ofosu-Amaah. "Ethical Aspects of Externally Sponsored Research in Developing Countries: An African Viewpoint." Bankowski, Z. and Howard-Jones, N. (eds.). *Human Experimentation and Medical Ethics*, (General: Council for International Organizations of Medical Sciences, 1982), pp.270–275.

[2]

Ian Smillie, *No Condition Permanent: Pump-Priming Ghana's Industrial Revolution*, (London: Intermediate Technology Publications, 1980), pp.36–7.

quotation. It would be, beyond any doubt, unethical to rob the LDC recipients of the initiative to promote their own development. Donor agencies need to look at particular ethical dilemmas not only at the level of individual activities (and this is sometimes well treated); but bearing in mind the criticisms above, there is a good case to be made about agencies being concerned about their general patterns of activity.

Much discussion, in the industrialized countries, has been devoted to the underlying rationale for Official Development Assistance (ODA). In Canada there has been, historically, a shifting emphasis between humanitarian and commercial objectives. Most studies of Canadian ODA arrive at a broadly similar conclusion—

the population generally supports the humanitarian objective of ODA, yet does not reject the possibility of its use to promote economic interests or influence abroad.[1] An agency which finances research for international development within this milieu is placed in the peculiar position of being accountable to the home population, while responding simultaneously to the needs expressed by those institutions in the developing world. The relatively different perceptions of "donor" and "recipient" become the focus of concern particularly with respect to the ethical or moral elements of the processes by which research is supported and undertaken.

Although this chapter deals specifically with the ethical issues surrounding research and technologies in the field of international development, it also provides insights into the broader issues pertaining to the ethics of research in general, as well as into the ethics of the application of such research.

We will begin by setting out briefly some of the conceptual aspects of "ethics" in relation to research for international development. We will subsequently look at the empirical dimension of ethics and research, largely based on the experience of Canada's International Development Research Centre (IDRC). A standard research protocol is presented, followed by a series of questions which attempt to reach beyond the conduct of research itself. The final section offers some concluding observations.

Ethics and Development: Minimizing the Human Cost

The term "ethics" is a normative and relative concept, often meaning different things to different people in different contexts. In a general sense, it is associated with the principles of conduct governing individuals, communities or entire societies. Most of the literature on this subject appears to understand ethics in this way. In some schools of thought, ethics is broadly defined, to the point that every question can become an ethical issue. This leaves us with so vast an array of interconnections that it would not be a practical tool for our purposes. For an issue to be ethical there must be a wide consensus within a community or society as well as an intrinsic element which touches on fundamental subject matter. For example, the statement "Mr. X should be Prime Minister" does not generally carry a strong ethical connotation, whereas, "We want a Prime Minister who cares about the poor" more likely does.

In this chapter, we consider that which is ethical (or moral) as pertaining to *what one believes ought to be*, as being distinct from the empirical dimension of *what one knows to be*. This is an important distinction because perceptions of "what ought to be " as being a desirable condition, are akin to a value judgement which may be projected. In a similar vein, the disciplines connected with international development deal with the processes by which people or communities attempt to transcend their existing condition, which for so many millions in LDCs is one of absolute poverty, to a condition they believe to be better. Development, in this sense, becomes an ethical construct.

See Réal Lavergne, "The Determinants of Canadian Aid Policy," (Ottawa: International Development Research Centre, mimeo, 27 April 1987).

Michael Todaro provides an additional perspective with this guiding ethic of development:

> Since concern with economic development in the Third World ultimately involves dealing with the abject poverty of more than two-thirds of the world's population, no humanely acceptable discussion of development can avoid the fundamental ethical issues embodied in the questions: What kind of development? For whom? And by what political and institutional mechanisms? The choice among ends and alternative means is a critical one, ... our basic proposition is that the major ethical (and practical) issue in development promotion is how to achieve development's tangible and authentic material benefits at minimum human cost and without destroying the human capacity to act freely and retain those values and institutions so central to its nonmaterial world. It is a difficult, some might say impossible, task but one that development economists neglect at their own ethical peril.[1]

"Ethics" pertains directly and indirectly to living beings, particularly humans. A concern is often triggered when identifiable individuals or groups of individuals are affected by some event. It must be emphasized that the "minimum human cost" is a key factor. Some principles from development economics may be useful to consider in this regard.

Many theoretical models have been put forward in an effort to assist decision-makers in designing and implementing public policy. Such models as the "welfare optimizing model" (maximum happiness for the maximum number of people), and the "satisficing" model (what is possible given the resources), combined with the notion of "Pareto optimality" (no one is made better off at the expense of others) would lead us to this conclusion—the search for optima is less practical than the search for solutions which are "good enough"; solutions which will command the necessary minimum of individual or community support while exacting the least possible cost, both in human and social terms. This "second-best" argument is sound both theoretically and practically since we live in a world where there are many constraints preventing complete efficiency (in the economic sense).

The ethical dimension of international development has sometimes been referred to as a type of "triage"—the sorting and allocation of treatment to patients, battle and disaster victims according to a system of priorities designed to maximize the number of survivors. As will be illustrated in the cases to follow, research for international development elicits these types of ethical questions for both the researcher and the beneficiaries of research.

Ethical Choice and Research: Skewing the Benefits to Those in Need

For the agency which supports research in developing countries there remains an obligation to put in place a set of administrative procedures and guidelines to review the ethical aspects of research proposals. The Ethics Review Committee of the International Development Research Centre (IDRC) was established for this purpose. The ethical considerations applied in their reviews are based on i) consultations with relevant experts, ii) various national and international guidelines, and iii) literature-generated by professional associations. These considera-

---

Michael Todaro. "Ethics, Values and Economic Development." K. Thompson (ed.) *Ethics and International Relations*, (Oxford: Transaction Books, 1985) pp.75–97.

BOX 1

Research Protocol: Some Ethical Considerations in the Support of Research in LDCs

- in experimental trials where humans are the subject of research there may need to be; *informed consent* where participatory techniques are used, steps taken to ensure *confidentiality of information*, and consider a *"duty to inform"* if during the course of research, sensitive information concerning the subject's welfare should arise (i.e. AIDS virus detection);

- in research of biomedical nature it will be necessary to:
   - i. examine health and safety factors (e.g. children, pregnant women);
   - ii. adhere to humanitarian objectives in cases where animal life is involved (i.e. genetic engineering);

- validation of methodology for objectivity in results (i.e. peer review);

- procedures for ethical review by recipient LDC institution.

---

tions are outlined in Box 1 above. It is important to note that discussions on any ethical issue which has been "flagged" by the Committee culminate, in many cases, in special provisions being included within the Memorandum of Grant Conditions which is developed in consultation with the recipient LDC institution and government. This is done with a view to protecting the rights of the subjects of IDRC-supported research.

Do the points illustrated in Box 1 represent an adequate range of considerations? If not, how much farther should the net be cast? On matters of general policy, the IDRC has to deal with these types of issues:

1. Research which is clearly counter to prevalent government policy (e.g. democratic participation in Argentina under the military junta, research within or about apartheid in South Africa);

2. Research in countries whose principal ideologies are very different from ours, but whose leaders appear genuinely to be acting in the public interest (e.g. Mugabe's Zimbabwe);

3. Research where there are questions of territorial or political legitimacy, yet there exists a clear need for investigation into the basic needs of these communities (e.g. the PLO, West Bank);

4. Research in countries where the ruling élite condones a disproportionate flow of rewards to narrower constituencies or commits acts deemed "unethical" under international law (e.g. Noriega's Panama, Marco's Phillipines).

While these issues are subject to discussion in various committees and at senior decision-making levels, intuitively, there cannot be an ethical debate on every project supported by the Centre. Clearly, no project should put humans at risk or in a situation where the risk is not understood. The Centre is cautious, for example, in its support for pharmaceutical research especially due to the stringent regulations at home. It would not be appropriate to introduce a product in the developing world which does not meet the standards of an industrialized country.

How far beyond research should an institution or individual researcher be sensitive to ethical concerns? Nigel Calder states: "there is nothing that [people] should not know, but some things they should not do with their knowledge."[1] Today we implicitly accept this view. The researcher has, in the past, placed more emphasis on the conduct of research than on the ultimate use of the technology generated. In the field of genetic engineering a plethora of concerns from the general to the specific are brought into play with respect to research application. This point of view is reflected in the way ethical concerns are treated in development research—often vigorously applied to ensure protection of the subjects of research.

There is still no comprehensive framework for researchers to judge the merits of their work. More important, at this stage, will be the admission that some applications should be encouraged and others discouraged, but also that the selection is likely to be controversial, culturally specific or politically sensitive. A well known example would be the marketing of the Nestle's baby food formula to mothers in developing countries which deprived many children of nutritious mother's milk and, moreover, put children at risk because much of the available water for the mixture was contaminated in some form or another. This raises the question of what access the LDC population has to the results of research, particularly when they have been the subjects.

Time horizons also play an important role in research application. A certain insecticide may have adverse long-term health and environmental effects, yet may be condoned on the grounds that killing mosquitos reduces the incidence of malaria. Short-term objectives in this case may be the overriding factor in determining use of the chemical. How far into the future do ethical responsibilities extend? A peasant farmer using slash and burn techniques in Brazil may have to shift the locus of operations every three years due to reduced capacity of the soil to support growth. If research yields a new crop variety which could be sustained over a six to eight year period, should it be applied knowing that there is an outer limit to its use and that the farmer's family would eventually have to move? Is it sufficient to mitigate as opposed to solving a problem?

At the other end of the spectrum, if we were to adopt a strict code which inhibited the adoption of technologies which bring about change, it would ironically result in the most unethical scenario—condemning the poor to perpetual poverty. A researcher would need to speculate on the distribution of costs and benefits of a particular technology change. Let us suppose that a research project produced a methane converter which is usable by individual households to serve energy needs such as cooking or lighting. A family which can efficiently collect dung from four cows, for example, would be able to develop a small household

---

Nigel Calder. *Technopolis: Social Control of the Uses of Science*, (New York: Simon & Schuster, 1970) p.353.

energy system. This type of project is appealing to the poorer segments of a Third World society. Yet in a country where entitlement to cows is restricted, these families may garner disproportionate access to the cows thus making more difficult the access for widows with no families to assist in the process. This example shows that when one attempts to confer a wide benefit, some segments of society will be disadvantaged even though the research proposal conforms to the definition of minimizing the human cost. Researchers will have to make judgments concerning the net overall benefits, and the distribution of such benefits. Would it be ethical to recognize the disadvantages created and put in place alternate programs for those negatively affected?

Another illustration raises questions of what expectations or level of understanding does a scientist need in adopting a full range of technologies, before ethically supporting the use of results. Since cassava is a staple food consumed by many families in LDCs, much research has been devoted to improving the properties of the plant. There is a growing body of evidence in medical research, however, that continued, high levels of cassava consumption may result in endemic goitre and cretinism among children. This is traceable to arsenic compounds in the cassava. Researchers have investigated various methods of treating the vegetable to reduce the levels of toxicity. This includes a very simple, low cost, but time consuming process of treating the cassava prior to consumption. There is doubt, therefore, as to how often the approach will be adopted by rural families, because of the time factor. What ethical obligation exists for the researcher?

To what degree should a researcher construct a hypothetical chain of events or counterfactual scenario in order to skew the benefits to those most in need? Fish attracting devices, which are the products of research designed to assist poorer sections of a fishing community, may have the effect of accelerating competition. The larger players could adopt "state-of-the-art" technology such as the "freezer trawler" which processes and packages fish on the spot. Apart from the increased potential for overfishing, does the research contribution make the poorer fisherfolk better off once the externalities are considered?

The Asian farmer referred to at the outset, in acquiring the technology package which is the result of some agricultural research, is situated at a crossroads. While the technology offered appears to widen the range of choices, all things considered, are we unwittingly putting him at risk of following a non-sustainable path?

Although the above examples are cast in the context of the world's poorer, underdeveloped societies, who comprise over two thirds of the global population, the overall ethical questions are applicable to the relationships between research, technology and ethics in general. All research and all technology have, one way or another, human consequences. If we substitute in our analysis, nuclear reactors and nuclear physics for the simpler technologies applied to the Third World, the relationship and logical structures remain the same.

Conclusion: A Caution to the Judge

The discussion presented thus far would lead us summarily to conclude that:

1. While one can construct a wide definition of "ethics," praxis in research requires consideration of the following elements:

BOX 2

Considerations during development of a research project

- clear identification of target beneficiaries
- comprehensive analysis of user and beneficiary needs
- participatory methodologies to transfer a sense of "ownership" of research outputs to users and beneficiaries
- strong project leadership
- well developed communications strategy

Elements of framework for the management of research technologies

- product/service
- user/adopter
- market potential
- economic and political environment
- distribution channels
- user/adopter behavior
- price/cost of final product

(a) what one believes ought to be versus what one knows to be;

(b) the search for optima is less practical than a "second best" solution; and,

(c) it is important to minimize, to the extent possible, the human and social costs

(d) there can sometimes be a system of priorities designed to maximize and skew the benefits to those most in need, yet there will almost always be some group or subgroup which is disadvantaged

2. The standard research protocol is sufficient for a "one-time" review of proposals. Beyond the research itself, however, there are many ethical questions about which researchers should be concerned. One such question pertains to the *uses* of research. In this connection there is an implicit understanding that there is nothing that people should not know, but there are some applications of knowledge which elicit an ethical concern. In addition to individual activities, participating agencies will need to be concerned about their general patterns of activity.

To serve as an illustration of the steps which could be taken to promote the utilization and management of research technologies, an operating framework is presented in Box 2. These general principles have been developed in consultation with scientists and research institutions both within LDCs and the industrialized world.

While there are ethical questions to be raised which are project or sector specific, a much larger concern exists. As Denis Goulet has noted in a study of value conflicts in the transfer of technology to LDCs:

> ... technology itself is a two-edged sword. It is simultaneously the bearer and destroyer of precious human values, bringing perhaps new freedom from old constraints and introducing new determinisms into the life of its adepts.[1]

He postulates that the basic values embodied in Western technology—the reductionistic and sometimes impatient approach to problem-solving, a profit maximizing calculus in its views on efficiency and productivity, and a view of the universe which sees nature and technology as objects to be used and manipulated—could serve to break down the very principles of cohesion in a non-Western society. Here, societies are faced with critical choices in determining the nature of the research required to help improve their existing condition. What do they really want?

Every value which is part of a cultural system cannot easily be handled by any cost-benefit formula. For research which is intended to benefit the marginal, resource-poor segments of society, how is one to determine what is the currency of happiness, or those conditions "which ought to be?" A telling reflection of the differences in visions of development is contained in a study undertaken at the University of Madras. Researchers initiated a survey of inhabitants of the slums within this South Indian city, to find out what were their actual priorities and needs. When asked what they desired most, if anything, the response was not exactly what one would expect. Instead of clean water, improved sanitary conditions or education programmes, most of the respondents expressed a desire for streetlighting. Two interesting points emerge. People in these communities are cognizant of the fact that not all of their immediate problems will be resolved through research, so their principal concern was to add some element of pleasure to their current state by extending their social life into the evening hours.

Even more revealing is this paraphrased but characteristic response from some LDC communities which have been the subjects of research:

> We are tired of so many people coming to study us and fill out questionnaires so they can write books and make themselves famous... Our members cannot read those books and our members had no choice but to respond when the researcher come to us.

There is perhaps a lesson in these experiences. To this effect Bernard Williams states:

> There is great pressure for research into techniques to make larger ranges of social values commensurable. Some of the effort should rather be devoted to learning—or

---

Denis Goulet. *The Uncertain Promise: Value Conflicts in Technology Transfer*, (Washington, D.C.: Overseas Development Council, 1977), p.17.

learning again, perhaps—how to think intelligently about conflicts of values which are incommensurable.[1]

What is required for the institutionalization of the principles of ethics is a learning environment. This is necessary to understand and to interpret the values of other cultures in an effort to resolve the conflicts and tensions which arise when technological change outpaces the institutional arrangements necessary to accommodate them. With the proliferation of modernizing values of the industrialized countries, many developing countries, which once may have had a deep sense of their own worth, wind up in a state of cultural confusion when they come in contact with the technologies of advanced societies. Because material prosperity is often equated with self-worth and esteem, those nations which are not economically and technologically powerful are somehow ashamed. Again, we quote Denis Goulet:

> As long as esteem or respect [is] dispensed on grounds other than material achievement, it [is] possible to resign oneself to poverty without feeling disdained... Nowadays the Third World seeks development in order to gain the esteem which is denied to societies living in a state of disgraceful "underdevelopment" ... Development is legitimized as a goal because it is an important, perhaps even an indispensable way of gaining esteem.[2]

As Ivan Head, President of IDRC has counselled on many occasions, development is, first and foremost, the pursuit of human dignity. The essential thing for research then, is humility in one's approach, a caution to the judge about his or her own behavior and attitudes.

JAMES MULLIN is Vice-President, Program at the International Development Research Centre (IDRC) in Ottawa, Canada.
ARUN ABRAHAM is his Research Associate.

The authors would like to acknowledge the assistance of Lise Vallee, Secretary.

---

[1]

Bernard Williams. *Morality: An Introduction to Ethics*, (New York: Harper and Row, 1972), p.97.

[2]

Quoted in M. Todaro *op.cit.* p.91–92.

UNIT VIII
CONSEQUENCES AND IMPLICATIONS

Technology and Marginalization

boriginal peoples the world over have lived on the margin between their traditional life-styles and so-called "technological development" for centuries. In that sense, they are in much the same position relative to technology and development as are the countries known as the "Third World."

One of my colleagues and a predecessor as President of the National Indian Brotherhood described the situation as thus: "The Fourth World has always been here in North America. Since the beginning of European domination, one by one, have been denied the light of day. Its fruit has been withered and stunted. Yet the tree did not die ... Our grandfathers faced and endured the physical violence of wars, famine, and disease. They survived ... Now there is the possibility that our grandchildren may yet face the danger of material success."[1]

As an aboriginal person of Canada, therefore, I can relate to Third World countries and appreciate their predicaments as they strive to keep up with the developed countries of the so-called First World to enjoy the material success of the twenty-first century.

In the Third World, technology is outdated and outmoded. Most of those countries are employing old technology, old hardware and old machinery. They want to acquire newer technologies from the developed nations in order to advance; and this results in their having to take on heavy debt burdens in order to pay for them. A vicious cycle then begins: unable to repay debts, needing new capital investment to catch up, lacking equity and collateral with which to balance off new loans and confronted by lenders who are not excited about financing them further, they find it virtually impossible to catch up. The Third World is therefore starved of financial resources, especially the concessional loans and grants which are most suitable to long-term developmental needs.

The debt crisis is starting to resemble the chaotic reparations situation in the aftermath of World War I which helped create the instability that led to World War II. According to the Canadian North-South Institute, Canadian companies are losing about $3.5 billion every year in export sales because of the mounting financial burden of Third World debt; and, by insisting on the sanctity of bankers' balance sheets, "we're turning yesterday's customers into today's beggars."

At the beginning of this decade, now almost at its end, the International Coalition for Development Action looked into the crystal ball of the eighties and

---

George Manuel and Michael Posluns *The Fourth World: An Indian Reality*, (Toronto: Collier Macmillan Canada Ltd., 1974).

saw that, "Developing countries are forced to borrow in the hope that future earnings will pay off the debt and leave sufficient surplus for investment. During the seventies, the debt of Third World countries more than tripled... For many countries export earnings have failed to rise as quickly as expected, while import costs have risen sharply. They now face a heavy debt-servicing burden, leaving next to nothing for vital development projects."[1]

In April 1989, the Declaration of Addis Ababa underscored the fact that the debt burden of 28 African countries had, indeed, more than tripled in the last decade amounting today to $40 billion. These facts, and others, clearly indicate that it is impossible for the Third World to catch up with the First World. The old form of marginalization simply becomes a new form of marginalization on a carousel of poverty, hopelessness and despair.

Energy

While the Third World grapples, ever more feebly, to secure and maintain basic services such as running water, sanitation and electricity, always trying to catch up, ever at the margin, the First World has the luxury of moving from one type of fuel to another.

The energy "gap" has already started a polarization in the First World industrial societies. Conventional plans to fill that gap by nuclear energy—from 3% to 20% by 1990—were attacked not only for their cost, danger and effect on the environment, but also as a leap forward to an over-centralized, automated and alienating world.

Decreasing the Margin

One way for us to start the long process of "demarginalization" is to support the indigenous peoples in their claims for land rights at the same time as we endorse their non-polluting activities on the land. In a real and practical way, the World Conservation Strategy[2] must be implemented. The only way by which the status quo with all its horrible portents for our future would be meaningfully ameliorated would be for environmentalists, rural people, farmers, fishermen and others like them to join with aboriginal peoples in becoming a serious part of a sustainable development strategy. Conservation has always been integral to the survival of aboriginal peoples. Without renewable resources to harvest, they lose both their livelihood and way of life. Aboriginal communities, in whatever part of the world they may be, have everything to gain from conservation—and much to offer: a profound and detailed knowledge of species and ecosystems; ways of sharing and managing resources that have stood the test of time; and ethics that reconcile subsistence and co-existence, recognizing that people are an integral part

---

[1]

Crisis Decade: The World in the Eighties, (International Coalition for Development Action, 1980).

[2]

Union for Conservation of Nature and Natural Resources, World Conservation Strategy, (1980).

of nature, and expressing spiritual bonds with other species, including those they harvest.

Conservation and development policy-making and planning often seem to assume that aboriginal peoples have only two options for the future: either to return to their traditional way of life, or to abandon subsistence altogether and become assimilated into the dominant society. Neither option is reasonable. They have a third option: to modify their subsistence way of life, combining the old and the new in ways that maintain and enhance their identity while allowing their societies and economies to evolve. As the original conservationists, they now aim to combine development and conservation, and put into practice the concept of equitable, culturally appropriate, sustainable development. As such, the goal of World Conservation strategy is their goal, too.

Sustainable Resources

Sustainable development means a shift of emphasis from non-renewable to renewable resources; yet, as we develop renewable resources we must not destroy or eliminate the non-renewable. It is imperative, for example, that we restore our forests.

The oldest ecosystem on our planet Earth, i.e. the rainforests, is to be found within a 3,200 kilometre band straddling the Equator. Being more lush and much denser than any other forests because of their heavy rainfall, they support an unparalleled biological diversity and richness. We are told that at least five million species—between 50 to 80 per cent of all living things—thrive there. Rainforests regulate our global climate by helping to control the greenhouse effect—the gradual warming of the Earth's atmosphere—and they also capture, store and recycle rain, prevent floods, drought and soil erosion.

Yet, only about 2.4 billion acres of rainforest are left in the world today, according to expert information. Humankind has successfully destroyed at least half the original acreage. Once again, the frontier mentality which exterminated thousands upon thousands of aboriginal peoples is at work in the Third World countries destroying "the lungs of our earth" at the rate of a hundred acres every minute!

Third World countries, which already live on the margin of international society, should no longer be pressured to cut down their rainforests for the sake of developmental funds. We must eliminate the notion that those areas exist simply for profit and then to benefit only a few; and stop racing to a future where every inch of our Earth is urbanized with factories, offices and skyscrapers without a tree or a plant anywhere. It is essential to our very survival as a species, for both those who live on the margin and those who benefit from the full bloom of the modern technological age, that we save the "green" areas of our global environment that are being destroyed by acid rain and other pollutants. Our global planning must include large green areas; and we must eliminate the notion that green areas are undeveloped and just waiting to be "developed."

Where conservation and environmental protection are concerned, aboriginal peoples stand second to none. Environmentalists should recognize that aboriginal peoples are their best allies in the task of conservation. As the World Commission on Environment and Development recognized in its 1987 Report, *Our Common Future*,[1] aboriginal peoples "are the repositories of vast accumulations of traditional knowledge with its ancient origins." Referring to isolated communities of aboriginal peoples, the Commission said, "[t]heir disappearance is a loss for the larger society, which could learn a great deal from their traditional skills in sustainably managing very complex ecological systems."

Being as they are on the margin—whether in developed or in developing countries—aboriginal peoples still have much to give to the world, by way of environmental protection and sustainable development. For many non-aboriginal persons, neither the individual nor the human community is viewed as a natural extension of the ecosystem. Consequently, the human element is ignored and plays no role in the so-called wilderness. The human species is elevated to a "sophisticated" level that is above wildlife and above his environment. Therefore, "conservation" has come to mean "nature without humankind." To the aboriginal person that is an aberration. That is why, situated as they are on the margin between technology and traditional lifestyles, aboriginal peoples are well placed to be in the vanguard of those defending the green area as an integral part of all cultural milieu.

Cultural Values

The importance of preserving traditional cultures cannot be over-emphasized. What is true for aboriginal peoples holds good for the Third World. As the International Coalition for Development Action recommended:

> … [t]he cultural and political components among basic needs are vitally important … Participatory patterns of democracy, and respect for the people's culture—their values, their language, their religious beliefs, their arts and crafts—must be preserved. Development has no meaning if people are alienated from the process of their environment which provides a richness to their lives. It is the erosion of their cultural values which has been taking place in the absence of a positive policy of self-reliance. A policy of self-reliance would seek to preserve cultural basic needs as well as providing material basic needs.[2]

As an indigenous person I could not agree more.

Pace of Development

The pace of technological and other modern development has to be challenged and arrested; it ought not to be maintained at the speed of the last two decades. If economic growth and profit margins remain the criteria by which we judge development, then underdevelopment and continued marginalization of the poorer nations and peoples will persist while the gap widens even further. Clearly, the free-enterprise economy, driven as it is by the profit motive, does not provide the

---

[1]

World Commission on Environment and Development, *Our Common Future*, (Oxford: Oxford University Press, 1987).

[2]

International Coalition for Development Action, *op.cit.*

solution largely because it ignores environmental needs and regional disparities. At the same time, experience shows that the totally-planned economy is not successful either.

What is required is a synergistic formula involving a new development paradigm which rethinks planning and investment. We have to find a way that enables the poorest among us—both nations and peoples—to be a part of and share equitably in the political and economic process. Moreover, we need to recognize not only the importance of our environmental resources but also the importance of human resources. Every effort should be made to stem the inflow of people from the rural areas or countryside to the towns and cities if we are to achieve a better balance of needs between rural and urban areas.

At the international level, efforts by the Third World to increase their own scientific and technological capacity are already underway but much of it is heavily dependent on First World financing thus further reinforcing dependency linkages to what has already been described as the "feudal" grip of the transnational corporations. In addition, the developed countries need to work with the Third World to resolve the debt burden of the latter as well as to help them acquire technology appropriate to their culture and *real* needs. Without these efforts at the international level and similar ones within nation-states, we cannot even begin to think of bridging the gap between rich and poor nations and rich and poor peoples whether in Canada or elsewhere.

GEORGE ERASMUS is Chief of the Assembly of First Nations, Ottawa.

23   *Jan Jørgensen*

Global Interdependence: Dimensions and Dilemmas

I t is possible to delineate several dimensions of global interdependence, each
providing a different slice of reality and framework for analysis. Six are
provided for illustration.

Six Dimensions of Global Interdependence

We live in an *ecologically* interdependent world where energy production in
one country contributes to acid rain, climatic changes, nuclear contamination, and
desertification elsewhere, a world where air-conditioning and plastic foam packaging deplete the ozone layer affecting life globally. Our current actions pose
monumental future problems, ranging from disposable diapers to nuclear and
chemical wastes.

Ours is a *technologically* interdependent world where repressive dictatorships
rely on imported weapons and technology, yet opposition dissidents occasionally
gain access to fax machines and desk-top publishing. Interdependence extends to
"soft" technology such as management know-how, which is often transferred with
little regard for differences in cultural contexts.

Global interdependence in *health* is demonstrated by the successful programme
to eradicate smallpox and the battle to slow the global spread of AIDS and
apportion its costs. Genetic engineering promises miracle drugs, but new drugs
are often discovered by testing plants and traditional medicines from the Third
World. Yet health in the Third World is placed at risk by pharmaceutical imports
banned in industrialized countries.

We live in a stratified world of *economically* interdependent nation-states, a
world in which the disparity in per capita income between rich and poor nations
exceeds forty to one. Yet within the richest nations some people are homeless or
unemployed, while within the poorest nations some drive Mercedes and employ
many servants. Meanwhile, the 1980s have witnessed massive net transfers of
funds from the Third World to industrialized countries. Debt servicing threatens
sustainable development in much of Latin America and Africa. Although the debt
crisis erodes the capital structure of our banks and export orders of our engineering
firms, it is the poor in the Third World who shoulder the brunt of adjustment rather
than shareholders of major banks in industrialized countries.

Ours is a *socially* interdependent world. Innuit and Cree hunters and trappers
can lose their meager livelihood not only because of hydro-electric projects for
the northeast United States but also because of the animal rights movement in
Europe. The publication of a novel in Britain can spark riots in Pakistan. Crime

in U.S. cities, assassinations in Colombia, money laundering in Toronto, dictatorship in Panama, and the trial of a military hero in Cuba are linked by the international drug trade.

We live in a *politically* interdependent world where security based on mutually assured destruction (MAD) is yielding to more positive concepts of common security. It is a paradoxical world where liberal democratic freedoms are in the ascendancy, yet the immediate fruits are often intense nationalistic strife. It is still a world where the political power needed to enjoy the "level playing field" of markets is severely malapportioned.

Inter-relatedness of Dimensions

The dimensions of global interdependence are themselves inter-related in unexpected ways. It was less than a decade ago that desk officers at governmental aid agencies scoffed at environmental and women's issues as mere fads of secondary importance to economic development. Research on the key role of women in development issues ranging from food production and population policy to trade and crafts has stilled critics. Moreover, this year environmental issues dominated the Paris summit of the seven leading western industrialized nations. In a similar vein, it is now academically respectable to conduct research on the links between ecology and international conflict in regions ranging from the Baltic to the Horn of Africa.

Dilemmas of Interdependence

Global interdependence gives rise to dilemmas, seven of which are discussed below. All involve ethical choices related to technology.

Inter-generational Interdependence and Entropy

Inter- generational transfers of wealth include natural resources, risk reduction, the ability to sustain development and service debt, infrastructure, culture and information, genetic pools of other species as well as our own, and the remaining pollution-carrying capacity of the planet.

In the market economy, individual and collective choices have been based on the belief that each generation has the right to maximize its own welfare, a view that Perelman has labelled "inter-generational libertarianism."[1] This view discards the entropic concept of irrevocability that flows from the Second Law of Thermodynamics. As Perelman observes, the source of a current problem may lie in the distant past and be insoluble by current means; the solution to a problem within one time frame may lead to catastrophic consequences in the longer run; and a current catastrophe may be the best route to a better future situation. Entropy leads to ethical choices:

Lewis J. Perelman, "Time in System Dynamics," *System Dynamics. TIMS Studies in the Management Sciences*, Vol. 14, edited by Augusto A. Legasto, Jr., Jay W. Forrester, and James M. Lyneis, (New York: North-Holland Publishing, 1980), p.79.

Our posterity is totally at our mercy; our every act may influence their fate. At the same time, it is their condition that imbues our own existence with purpose.[1]

Therefore, even the specification of a time frame to evaluate alternative outcomes involves ethical choice.

Individual Choice and Economizing on Death

At a 1987 conference, social scientist, James March enraged his audience by insisting that most decisions had some lethal consequences. Should one wear cotton that depletes the soil or fur that involves killing animals or shoes made of leather? For large-scale energy needs should one choose coal, petroleum, or nuclear fuel? Apart from mining accidents, coal exposes miners to radon gas and adds to acid rain and greenhouse effects. Petroleum extraction involves inevitable oil platform and tanker accidents and shares coal's negative climatic effects. Nuclear fuel shoves waste problems onto future generations. At best one could try to economize on the death caused by one's consumption and other choices, but March argued that the calculations themselves were paralyzingly complex.

The informational if not the ethical problems in individual choice could be lessened if firms were forced to move to what is called full cost pricing. The cost of a newspaper, or cereal packaging would include the cost of reforestation and waste removal and other negative externalities which might currently be shoved onto government bodies. Imagine what full-cost pricing might do to the cost of the Sunday *New York Times*, to nuclear power, or to the family car, the "sacred cow" of North America.[2]

Biased Rationality: Masculine Science

The scientific tools for studying global problems may be seriously flawed. As Brock-Utne states, "Masculine science, epitomized by Francis Bacon, implies mastery of man over nature. Feminine science, epitomized by Plato, implies that humans are a part of nature."[3]

The world is *sexually* globally interdependent. As a species we share a common ancestry. The traditional sexual division of labour in which men played a minor role in child rearing has encouraged men to glorify power over others including nature. This has in turn led to subtle biases in science and engineering which may hamper the search for solutions. Brock-Utne offers anecdotal evidence that scientists have neglected solar power as an alternative energy source because the problem is not deemed sufficiently challenging.

It is less clear how to proceed to correct such biases in the sciences. Should one seek to alter the valuation of what is "good science" or should one first seek to

---

[1]
  Ibid., p.83.

[2]
  Marvin Harris, "Mother Cow." *Cows, Pigs, Wars, and Witches; Riddles of Culture*, (New York: Random House, 1974), pp.11–32.

[3]
  Birgit Brock-Utne, "Formal Education as a Force in Shaping Cultural Norms Relating to War and the Environment," pp.83–100 in Westing, Arthur H. *Cultural Norms, War and the Environment*, (Oxford: Oxford University Press for Stockholm International Peace Research Institute and United Nations Environment Programme, 1988), p.88.

redistribute societal child rearing tasks to inculcate more nurturing and less conquering attitudes toward nature?

Nationalism and the "Selfish Gene"

According to journalist Gwynne Dyer, nationalism and the lack of altruism toward strangers has its biological roots in the genetic code because it has in the past been functional for survival of genetic material. Under the threat of a nuclear winter destroying the human race, the "selfish gene" has become dysfunctional. Fortunately, humans can rise above genetically instinctive behaviour when faced with a compelling reason to do so, and we are witnessing significant reduction in tensions among the major powers but simultaneously we are witnessing a resurgence of vitriolic nationalism in many corners of the world.[1]

From Self-Reliance to Sustainable Development and Back?

As the nostrum of the 1970s, self-reliance has become somewhat passé, quite deservedly so considering the varying degrees of stagnation that resulted from its pursuit in Tanzania, Burma and Albania. Part of the attraction of sustainable development in the 1980s is the image of global economic participation. Barbie dolls are produced for North American children by sub-contractor manufacturing plants in China. But sustainable development may simply evade two unresolved issues of the 1970s: the problem of unequal exchange and the question of whether the global system is open or closed.

The international politics of subsidized beet sugar shutting out cane sugar from the Third World and the unequal burdens imposed by the Third World debt crisis attest to the continued problem of unequal exchange. A major assumption underlying both Wallerstein's world system and the Club of Rome "limits to growth" model is that, in the short-run and quite possibly the long-run, the capitalist world economy is essentially a zero-sum game. Despite growth, there is at any point a finite pie to be divided and that one group's gain is another's loss.

Nevertheless, expansion of the size of the pie through economic growth can mitigate conflicts over its apportionment. The more fundamental question is whether expansion of the pie can continue indefinitely. For different reasons, both Wallerstein and the Club of Rome said the answer was no. Ultimately the system was closed and would exhaust the supply of resources needed for growth (new territories or pre-capitalist formations into which to expand in the case of Wallerstein, natural resources and global carrying capacity for the Club of Rome). Sustainable development offers a vision of an open system in which growth can continue at least into the early 21st century.

But if the system is closed in the long run, we may need to resurrect self-reliance with its associated bleak growth prospects. Even in the short run, a measure of self-reliance may be needed by developing countries to alleviate the risks associ-

---

[1]   Gwynne Dyer, "Has Humanity Reached the Age of Rationality? " *Montreal Gazette*, July 10, 1989, p.B–3.

ated with unequal exchange. Cheng has drawn a parallel between firms that vertically integrate and countries that pursue self-sufficiency to reduce uncertainty.[1] The uncertainty argument for self-reliance is less strong for industrialized countries. First, greater diversification offers greater opportunities for off-setting risks. Second, specialization among industrialized nations is largely within industries rather than between industries. Because it is easier to shift resources within industries than between industries, a country with firms in each key industry faces lower risks in responding to changing international conditions than one with "missing" industries. Third, major industrial nations have greater retaliatory economic power to deter economic strategic moves by other nations. For example, in 1980 even Australia was as large a trading country as China.

Transfer of Technology Across Cultures

Studies of technology transfer have shown that technology is like a fragment of a broken hologram. Each fragment is capable of reproducing the whole image. A piece of machinery is not an inert neutral object. Instead its design and plan of use carries with it the image of a larger social fabric and social order with assumptions about the division of labour and control of labour.[2] So the transfer of "hard technology" requires adaptation to the culture of the recipient.

If we turn to soft technology transfer such as the transfer of western management expertise to developing countries, then the need for adaptation is even greater. What is less clear is where the responsibility for adapting technology lies. There are at least three views on the subject:

According to one view, transfer without adaptation by the exporter is at best arrogant and at worst a form of cultural imperialism. If the transfer involves sending Westerners to developing countries, such experts have an obligation to be "polite guests." Rather than criticize or attempt to overhaul the values and social framework they find, they should work to adapt their expertise to serve the goals of their host country.

Another view holds that adaptation by the exporter also involves risks and arrogance. An analogy might be drawn from cooking. If a Canadian chef is invited to China to teach Canadian cuisine, would it not be presumptuous for the chef to attempt to adapt the recipe to Chinese tastes, resulting in a mishmash that is neither Canadian nor Chinese? Far better according to this school, to teach pure Canadian cuisine, and let the Chinese borrow and adapt as and if they wish.

A third view minimizes the need for any adaptation of the management know-how itself, it is the receiving society which must be adapted to fit the know-how. Cultural and political factors in the receiving society that differ from those in the technology exporting society are anachronisms which must be eradicated to have a universally valid economic structure. Here one finds the

---

[1]

Leonard Kwok-Hon Cheng, *A Market Failures Approach to International Trade and Specialization*, (Berkeley: University of California, unpublished doctoral dissertation, 1980).

[2]

Frederic J. Fleron, Jr., "Afterword." *Technology and Communist Culture: The Socio-Cultural Impact of Technology under Socialism*, (New York: Praeger, 1977), pp.457–487.

so-called convergence hypothesis that technological diffusion ultimately leads to a uniform societal and organizational culture.

Markets versus Hierarchies

The final point is that global society today consists increasingly of markets and organizations, two alternative forms for allocating resources and coordinating tasks. Research in management has focused recently on the choice between markets and hierarchies (organizations and governments) to achieve goals. The research involves judgements about effectiveness and efficiency, performance criteria which require ethical choices.

The market is in vogue this decade as witnessed by the global fashion of privatization. Yet we need both markets and hierarchies, and it is necessary to avoid a stylized opposition of the two forms. If we leave everything to market decisions then the main franchised group in society will be shareholders of large firms with market power. If we rely increasingly on organizations to solve problems, often created by organizations, then we risk enfranchising only analytical whiz-kids with MBAs who lack wisdom[1] and have a mute sense of ethics. Finally, Walter Powell has written on hybrid organizational arrangements such as networks which may serve as alternatives to both markets and hierarchies in the search for sustainable development.[2]

In conclusion, as global interdependence has grown since nation-states first emerged within a world market, so have the dimensions of interdependence become more varied and interrelated, recasting old dilemmas and revealing new ones. The scope for sustainable development depends less on technology and planetary constraints, important as these may be, than on individual and collective ethical and political choices. For these, we need self-imposed constraints on accumulation in order to allow more widely shared opportunities for creativity and self-actualization, both globally and across generations.[3]

DR. JAN JØRGENSEN is Professor of Policy Studies, Faculty of Management at McGill University, Montreal.

Further Reading

Brown, Lester R., and 8 co-authors. *State of the World, 1989; A Worldwatch Institute Report on Progress Toward a Sustainable Society* (New York: W.W. Norton & Company, 1989).

Myers, Norman, with Uma Ram Nath & Melvin Westlake. *Gaia, An Atlas of Planet Management* (Garden City, NY: Anchor Press/Doubleday, 1984).

---

[1]

Henry Mintzberg and Jan Jørgensen (1987) "Emergent Strategy for Public Policy," *Canadian Public Administration*, 30 (2): 214–229.

[2]

Walter W. Powell, "Hybrid Organizational Arrangements: New Form or Transitional Development?" *California Management Review*, 29 (no.9, 1987): 67–87.

[3]

Jack N. Behrman, *Industrial Policies, International Restructuring and Transnationals*, (Lexington, Mass.: Lexington Books, 1984), pp.241.

Wallerstein, Immanuel. *The Capitalist World-Economy* (Cambridge: Cambridge University Press, 1979).

Westing, Arthur H. *Cultural Norms, War and the Environment* (Oxford: Oxford University Press for Stockholm International Peace Research Institute and United Nations Environment Programme, 1988).

World Commission on Environment and Development [Gro Harlem Brundtland Commission]. *Our Common Future* (Oxford and New York: Oxford University Press, 1987).

ETHICS AND TECHNOLOGY:
Ethical Choices in the Age of Pervasive Technology
A World Conference
University of Guelph
October 25-29, 1989

Conference Chair: Henry Wiseman

Co-Sponsors: The University of Guelph; Alcan Aluminium Ltd.;
Atomic Energy of Canada; Canadian International Development
Agency; Canadian Institute for International Peace and Security; The
Corporation of the City of Guelph; Communications Canada; Du
Pont Canada Ltd.; International Development Research Center;
Medical Research Center; Ontario Ministry of Energy; Ontario
Ministry of Agriculture and Food; Royal Society of Canada; Science
Council of Canada; Social Science and Humanities Research
Council; The Toronto Dominion Bank; UNESCO Paris.

Benefactors: Department of Justice, Ottawa; Ontario Institute for
Studies in Education; Wageningen Agricultural University, The
Netherlands.